AGAINST ALL ODDS
PIONEERS OF SOUTH AMERICA

Against All Odds

PIONEERS OF SOUTH AMERICA

BY MARION LANSING

Illustrations by WILLIAM SHARP

Essay Index Reprint Series

BOOKS FOR LIBRARIES PRESS
FREEPORT, NEW YORK

STANDARD BOOK NUMBER:
8369-1149-0

LIBRARY OF CONGRESS CATALOG CARD NUMBER:
78-84318

PRINTED IN THE UNITED STATES OF AMERICA

To

Whether in North or South America

Preface

⋯⟩⫘⟩◉⟨⫘⟨⋯

EARLY AMERICANS WERE ALL PIONEERS. THEY CAME TO a New World and opened it up. In this experience they became Americans, creating a new pattern of life even while they kept much of the Old World pattern. As we follow the pioneers, we see peoples and nations in the making.

The experiences of the men who explored and developed South America were like those with which we are familiar on our Northern continent. Yet they are different, and therefore fascinating. The South American continent was so tremendous; the mountains were so high, the rivers so mighty, the plains so wide, the jungles so deep; and the problems, for these and a score of other reasons, were so great. Still the answers have been according to our own ways. Gauchos appeared on the pampas, as cowboys did on our Western plains. The urge for freedom grew, and the colonists fought to throw off overseas control. The patriots started to build republics, and there came to be separate nations, not states in a united republic as in the North. But soon these republics were united by roads and railroads, the telegraph and the airplane.

The challenge of a New World does something to the men who can meet it. Adventure becomes heroic, as men overcome all obstacles, triumph against all odds. So these pioneer stories belong not only to all South Americans, even though some are connected with only one region, but also to all Americans. They are a Pan-American inheritance which we cannot afford to miss.

Only a few pioneers can be chosen from an unending list. Those few are selected because they are outstanding and because they make a definite contribution to the life of today. Yet they may succeed in giving the spirit of them all.

In a field of history which parallels our own so closely and yet is unfamiliar, there is a natural curiosity about the sources for these brief biographies. For the El Dorado stories we are indebted to the Spanish chronicles and to the delightful volumes of R. B. Cunninghame Graham and John Augustine Zahm, whose works are classics which all readers would enjoy. For Father Fritz there are brief items in various reports, especially in an account of expeditions into the Valley of the Amazons, edited by Clements Markham for the Hakluyt Society. In a book published in 1816 John Mawe tells of his *Travels in the Interior of Brazil, Particularly in the Gold and Diamond Districts . . . by authority of the Prince Regent of Portugal, 1812*, an account matched by a still older volume entitled *A Succinct Abridgment of a Voyage Made within the Inland Parts of South America . . . as read to the Academy of Sciences, Paris, April 28, 1745, by Monsieur Charles Marie de la Condamine*. There is, likewise, the *Notes of a Botanist* by Richard Spruce, published in London in 1894. Charles Darwin tells of his adventures in *The Voyage of the Beagle*, and Santos-Dumont of his life in his book *My Airships*. A contemporary account of the work of Wheelwright was published in 1877, *The Life and Industrial Labors of William Wheelwright in South America*, by Juan Bautista Alberdi, with an introduction by Caleb Cushing, a biography supplemented from many New England and South

American sources, among them Claude Fuess's *Men of Andover*.

For national figures like Bolívar, San Martín, O'Higgins, and Sarmiento, and for background material in both Spanish and English, the sources are too numerous to mention. In accounts of railroad building, steamboats, and airplane travel, as for many other phases of life, we are deeply indebted to articles in the *Pan American Union Bulletin*, and in particular for tributes here and in contemporary issues of the *Scientific American Supplement* on the life and work of Oswaldo Cruz. Nor would any list of acknowledgments be complete without reference to the courtesies extended by the Harvard University Library and the Boston Athenaeum.

To the printed words Mr. William Sharp has contributed greatly with maps and pictures. Even a casual glance at the distances covered by the earlier pioneers adds to the sense of wonder at their accomplishments. It is our hope that the South American scene may become through these too brief biographies more real, more vivid, and less remote.

M. F. L.

Cambridge, Massachusetts
August, 1942

Contents

AGAINST ALL ODDS

PIONEERS OF SOUTH AMERICA

El Dorado, the Gilded King

A STORY THAT OPENED UP A CONTINENT

IT WAS IN THE YEAR 1535, THREE YEARS
after the coming of the Spaniards to Peru, that a wandering Indian brought to Quito, northern capital of the
conquered Inca empire, the tale of El Dorado.

"In the place from which I come," he remarked to
one of the soldiers, "there is a king who covers his
body with gold, as other men cover themselves with
clothes."

3

The words were repeated to Sebastián de Belalcázar, one of Pizarro's lieutenants, who was in command at the Inca town at the moment.

"Bring the man to me," said Belalcázar. "Let him tell this tale to me."

So the stranger was brought before the Spanish governor and repeated his story.

"The king of my country," he said, "covers his body with gold as if it were a coat. Each morning he has himself rubbed over from head to foot with a sweet-smelling, sticky gum. Then there is spread over this a coating of gold, so that he shines as he walks."

Belalcázar listened and could not believe that he heard rightly. He called in his native interpreter, an Inca youth who knew the Spanish speech quite well, to make sure that he was understanding the man's words.

"Does he say 'gold'?" he asked. "Does he not mean a yellow paint or dye that looks like gold?"

The Spaniards had seen such treasures as they had never imagined in the temples and palaces of the Incas: gold plate, and ornaments, and carvings, and temple pieces. But gold so abundant that it was worn as a covering! That was a greater marvel.

The Inca lad repeated the governor's question, and the Indian shook his head.

"No," the boy reported, "it is not a dye from a plant. It is *de oro* that he means, golden, a coat of gold."

"Ask him how this can be, for gold is a rock that is dug out of the ground," said Belalcázar, to test the man further. "Tell him that I do not believe him."

But the stranger Indian insisted more emphatically. He shut his hand as if he were holding something in it and then pounded it with the other hand, repeating the word which the interpreter said meant, in his speech, "gold."

"He says it is pounded, broken up," the boy explained, feeling for the Spanish words. "It is all made small like—like salt." He brought out the last word triumphantly. Now his master would understand what was meant.

"Gold dust," said Belalcázar under his breath, and then aloud, pretending indifference, "Very well. Tell him that I shall ask others about this fairy tale that he is telling me. If he is not telling the truth, I shall have him punished severely."

But when the question was put to other Indians they, too, knew the story. Yes, they said, there was a king up north somewhere who covered himself with gold. They did not seem to care very much, and the governor was suspicious, wondering if they were concealing something. But perhaps it was part of their strange lack of interest in gold. The Spaniards could never understand why the natives did not value their gold more highly, and the Indians did not see why these all-powerful foreigners got so excited over a yellow rock, beautiful though it was, that could be dug out of the ground or found along the riverbanks. No, these men told the governor, they had never seen this king, nor did they know where he lived. But they had heard about him, and it was many days' journey away.

"Does he do this every day?" Belalcázar asked.

Some nodded. Others shook their heads.

"We do not know," said one.

"As I heard, it was only once in a while," added another.

Then a young Inca chieftain, who had been listening to this servants' talk, spoke.

"It is only a story," he declared scornfully. "Those people up north are jealous of the power and wealth of our Inca, who is the greatest and richest ruler in the world. They have spread this tale to make their king seem a great man, too."

At last there was found in the Inca temple an aged priest who knew the story well. He was so old and feeble that he could not go to Belalcázar, but the governor went to the inner temple to see him. He had been brought to Quito in his boyhood from a place three days' journey to the north, when the Inca had conquered his tribe. He recalled the story of this inland people as he had heard it from his grandfather.

"This is a part of their religion," he said, "and they keep it secret. This El Dorado, this Golden Man, goes once a year to an inland lake to offer sacrifices. He and his people worship the Devil and fear him above all living things. So once a year they bring rich treasures of gold and silver and emeralds to appease him."

"What of this story of the king's being covered with gold?" asked Belalcázar. It was that for which he cared, not for talk of which god these heathen savages worshiped.

"That is part of the story," replied the aged priest, thinking in his heart how silly these rude barbarians from across the waters were to be so greedy. "On the great holiday of the year, when these people come together from all over their region and meet at the lake's shore, their priests anoint their king's body with oil and spread it over with gold. So my grandfather used to tell it to me, when I was a little boy."

"What did the king do with this gold?" the Spaniard questioned. "Did he keep it on until it was rubbed off?"

"Oh, no. It was a part of the worship. While the king was being clothed in gold, the people were placing their treasures on a *balsa*, a reed boat. They brought so many that the boat was loaded almost to the water's edge. Then the king stepped aboard and floated the boat out to the center of the lake. All the people stood on the shore around the lake and shouted and played on their horns and pipes and drums, while the king threw all the treasure into the lake and then plunged in himself. Thus he washed away in the deep waters the gold with which he had covered his body, and so the evil spirits that lived in the lake were appeased."

Sebastián de Belalcázar went out from the temple with his eyes big and his breath coming fast. If only he could find that king, he might come into possession of wealth such as that which Cortés had seized from Montezuma and Pizarro was holding so greedily at the Inca capital at Cuzco! Or if there were no such king, he might locate the lake and drain off its waters and recover the treasure which had been dropped there for so many years.

He called the first Indian to him again.

"Where does that king of whom you told me live, and what is the name of the lake where he makes his sacrifices?" he asked.

"The lake is called the Lake of Guatavita," the man replied, "and the name of the country is Cundinamarca, and it is not more than twelve days' distance from here."

(Twelve days! It was to be more than twice twelve months before these Spaniards came to that country.)

Belalcázar went back to his quarters and told the story to his companions.

"Let us go in search of that Gilded Man!" they cried, or as one of their chroniclers, who wrote his history in rhyme, has given their words:

> *Ours be his gold and his pleasures;*
> *Let us enjoy that land, that sun!*

The story of El Dorado, the Gilded Man, crossed the ocean and was repeated in the courts of Europe and England. It was believed by kings and queens, soldiers and adventurers. For a hundred and more years men organized expeditions to find him. They explored the Amazon River, hoping to find the king and his treasure in the jungles. Sir Walter Raleigh came from England and journeyed up the Orinoco River, searching for an El Dorado which he believed to be a golden city. By the time the search was over, the continent had been crossed from west to east and east to west. South America had been opened up.

The first to follow the El Dorado trail were Belalcázar and his men. Yet when they came to that country of which the wandering Indian had told, they found that they were not alone in their search.

Three
Treasure Hunters Meet

THE MOST EXTRAORDINARY HAPPENING
IN ALL EXPLORATION

·····>·──◆>●<◆──·<····

IT COULDN'T HAPPEN—BUT IT DID! THAT
is all that can be said about the meeting of three exploring parties on the plain of Bogotá in the year 1538.

If the leaders had known the geography of the
country and planned to meet in a certain week at this
spot far in the interior of northern South America,
they could hardly have managed it so neatly. At least
one of them would have been late for the appointment,

for each party had been on its way for months or years, and not one of them knew the route or their destination, except that it was the home of the people ruled by the Golden King, that monarch who clothed himself in gold dust and then washed it off as carelessly as if it were dirt.

The place where they met (the present capital of Colombia) is higher than are the peaks of most mountains. It is a mile and a half above sea level and is walled in by higher mountains. Even in modern times this region is difficult of approach, a city set apart from the rest of the world. In those early days the Chibcha kingdom was as separate from the other peoples of South America as if it were set on an island; more separate, for mountain and jungle and forest are a more effective barrier than the sea.

No one of these parties knew of the existence of the others. They came from the north, the south, and the east, and each resented bitterly the presence of the others. Yet to this place they came, drawn by the lure of gold as by a magnet.

I

The exploring party that arrived first was led by a Spanish lawyer, the most interesting of the three leaders, Don Quesada, or, to give him his full name and title, Don Gonzalo Jiménez de Quesada.

He had never intended to be an explorer. The son of a distinguished lawyer, he was practicing law with his father in a city of southern Spain in the year 1535. But adventure was in the air. The news of the rich empires discovered by Cortés in Mexico and Pizarro in Peru had excited everyone. As one writer of the time puts it, "even the tailors wanted to go a-conquering, and looking out for mines."

Great expeditions were being sent out to occupy the regions so newly discovered across the sea, and Quesada was invited to join one of the most important of them. He was to be "chief magistrate" of the town of Santa Marta on the Caribbean coast, under a new governor who was going out for the first time.

The town of Santa Marta was found, when the fleet of ships with its thousand men and women arrived, to be no town at all. The colonists had expected a place where they could at least be comfortable. Here was only a miserable little village of mud huts, with a few thatched houses and a tumble-down church. Most of the newcomers had to live in tents. There was much sickness among them, and an atmosphere of gloom prevailed in the colony. It was not for this that they had crossed the seas.

The only remedy was to do some exploring and find gold. The reports from Mexico and Peru had set the standard. Some of the famed inland regions, about which such stories were told, must be discovered and conquered.

The governor sent out a company of men under his son, and they succeeded in finding, not too far away, an Indian town with a considerable store of gold in its temple and tombs. But the young leader was too much tempted by his find. He appropriated the treasure, hurried back to the coast, and hailed a passing ship, making good his escape to Spain, to the shame and grief of his distinguished father. The next searching party must be well commanded, by a man of unquestioned character. The governor's choice fell, not on one of the military men of the company, as would have been expected, but on Gonzalo de Quesada. In the few weeks since they had left the home country the lawyer had shown qualities of leadership which made him stand out among his fellows.

To us of later times there is something utterly unbelievable about the manner in which these sixteenth-century adventurers sallied forth on their expeditions across the ocean or into the unknown wilderness. The Santa Marta company had come clad in silks and satins and expecting to enter at once on a life not unlike that which they had left behind in Spain. Now Quesada's exploring expedition set forth as if for a conquering march over open territory with navigable rivers, a gay and gallant company of 600 foot soldiers, 200 sailors, for the five boats, and 100 horses.

Their troubles began before they left the coast. At the mouth of the Magdalena one boat was wrecked on the sand bars. Two smaller vessels managed to enter the river, but the other two sailed off along the coast to Cartagena, where the crews deserted. Quesada and his associates had to buy and outfit three old boats, to replace these stolen craft, before the expedition could get fairly under way.

Then began one of the most difficult marches in all the history of exploration. Even in our own twentieth century the journey up the Magdalena is slow and far from easy. Quesada and his men met obstacles along every one of the five or six hundred miles.

The river was in flood, and the banks were swampy jungles through which the foot soldiers must struggle. The Spaniards seized the food of the natives, and the natives retaliated by attacking from canoes hidden in the high vegetation, shooting poisoned arrows at them. In order to make any progress, they had to take their axes and cut their way along the riverbanks. Quesada left the boat and went ashore and took his turn at chopping, to encourage his men. They tried to sleep in hammocks slung under the trees, and wild beasts attacked them. There were alligators in the waters and snakes in the grasses. The rains fell without a day's respite, and the men took sick with fever.

The expedition broke up into different parties, some going by water and others by land, and still the march went on. Weeks upon weeks came and went, until it was eight months since they had left the coast. Scores of men had died; others had been sent back by boat. There came a day when those who remained insisted that they should turn back, declaring that soon no one of them would be left alive. But Quesada showed them that to go on was their only hope. They could never survive the return journey in their weakened, starved condition.

So, at long last, they came to the edge of a rich, fertile, inland plain. Here there were villages where there was food, maize and other grains and root vegetables, to save them from starvation. There was still a last mountain wall to be ascended, and only the stronger of the survivors were equal to the climb. These men and their sixty horses pushed their way up the steep slopes of the Opon Mountains, into a region of intense cold for which they were wholly unprepared. Twenty men died there, but the rest pressed on, and

from the heights to which they came, exhausted, they
looked down on a wide, beautiful, fertile plateau, where
the Chibcha nation was living in peace and comfort.

"A goodly land! A land of plenty! A land of gold!"
the men shouted, almost out of their heads with joy
at the sight. But of the 800 who had started from Santa
Marta only 166 had survived to claim this reward.

"The Valley of Palaces," Quesada called it, as he
looked down on the many towns and villages. There
were no stone houses here, but round houses built of
wood and mud, with cone-shaped roofs thatched with
palm leaves. From the height these villages looked to
the Spaniards finer than they really were. They were
surrounded by high stockades, above which towered
tall poles, painted bright red, which stood at the street
corners and in front of the chiefs' houses.

Yet these people, the Chibchas, numbering well over
a million souls, were a nation with a high civilization,
as aboriginal life is reckoned. Not necessarily equaling
the Incas to the south or the Aztecs or Mayas to the
north, they were a peace-loving, agricultural people,
well governed and possessing much wealth.

The tale of the next few months is a sorry one. There
is the usual record of theft and cruelty and murder, of
betrayal of native chiefs and seizure of their possessions.
Quesada found the famous lake of El Dorado legend,

Lake Guatavita, a lonely spot far up in the hills. He heard stories of the ceremony which took place there every year, not a national celebration, but a local festival of only one of the Chibcha tribes. The true worship of the nation was a nature worship, connected with seed-sowing and harvests, for which the blessing of the gods was sought. But there were many ceremonies within the year, and one of these was held at this lonely little lake. The happenings were much as they had been described to Belalcázar by the wandering Indian. But here Quesada, as he heard the story, was given the reason for the ceremony. A chieftain's wife had drowned herself with her child, some said to get away from the chieftain. But he wanted her back, and a magician had told him to tempt her by gifts. So he poured out his gold and treasure each year into the waters. That, it was said, was the way the custom started. Then it was done each year by the chieftain of the tribe and came to be a religious ceremonial of purification and offerings to the gods. Such was the origin of the tale which was to sweep over all Europe.

There was gold in the region and gold in the Chibcha palaces, or such a story could never have started. Quesada and his men seized it and felt rewarded for all the hardships they had suffered. But the invaders did not get it all. The head of the Chibcha nation, the

great Bogotá, left his town and escaped into the mountains—so the story goes—accompanied by a long train
of servants who carried the nation's gold and other
treasures on their backs. It was buried, by his orders,
in secret places. He was killed, but that wealth the
Spaniards never found. Nor has the lake ever yielded
any great store of treasure, though it has been drained
several times in the centuries.

Then Bogotá's town, Muequeta, was burned. When
the Chibchas saw that they could not defend it they
shot arrows of blazing straw into the thatched roofs.
To its site, on a day that has been remembered and
celebrated for four hundred years, August 6, 1538, the
Spanish lawyer-conqueror summoned his captains and
soldiers, and with them many of the Chibchas who had
been forced to come under his rule. Beside the heap
of ashes of the old town, on this beautiful plain backed
by purple mountains, with snowy peaks beyond them
in the distance, Quesada had chosen to found his new
city. With a homesick memory of his youth, he named
the country New Granada, for its likeness to his faraway Granada in Spain. To his town he chose to give
the name of its fallen chief, Bogotá.

Like all the Spanish conquistadors, Quesada loved
a ceremony. With his audience of Spaniards and wondering Chibchas looking on, he rode his horse around

the chosen spot, then dismounted and plucked from the ground a tuft of grass. Slashing the earth three times with his sword, he cried: "I take possession of this land in the name of the most serene Emperor, Charles V."

Remounting his horse, he continued: "And I challenge to single combat, either on horseback or afoot, any who deny this right."

No man in that company raised his voice. In the silence that followed, Quesada sheathed his sword and, lawyer-fashion, bade his notary draw him up a deed to the site, which was signed by some of the onlookers as witnesses. Then he rode around the area again, marking out the places for twelve houses to be set in a circle, the twelve in memory of the twelve apostles, with a space left in the center for a church. The city of Bogotá, capital of the future republic of Colombia, had been founded. (Its four hundredth anniversary was celebrated in 1938.)

The ceremony over, Quesada began to plan for his journey homeward to report his act to his king in Spain. But while he delayed, following up a rumor of another El Dorado (this time not a Golden Man, but a Golden House, filled with more treasure than any man had ever seen), there came disturbing news from the south.

If ever a challenge had seemed safe, it had been that

one which Quesada flung to the winds as he circled the site of his future city. But one day a friendly Indian rode into the Spanish camp with startling news.

"Other white men are coming up from the south," he said, "men looking like you, but with better clothes and finer armor, and riding on fatter horses."

II

Three years had passed since Sebastián de Belalcázar heard in the Inca city of Quito the story of the Gilded Man who lived in the north. In his journey to that lonely lake of treasure he had crossed the Cordilleras, that chain of mighty mountains, ranging from ten thousand feet high and upward, which lay between the Pacific coast and the inland regions of the present republic of Colombia.

The journey had been one of frightful hazards. Belalcázar and his men had climbed to high mountain passes and made their way through them on narrow paths that hung over deep defiles. Coming down on the other side, they had spent weeks wandering in the lowlands, through dense forests and tropical jungles. Much of their travel had been through regions uninhabited even by the Indians, where there was neither food nor shelter for man or beast. The march was one of sharp contrasts. At one time the explorers would be suffering from the sticky, malarial heat of the jungle; and then, within a few days, they would be forced to march up into high regions where a sharp, intense cold pierced to the marrow of their bones. Such experiences tried men's souls.

They won through to the pleasant tablelands of Paéto and Popayán and stopped to make their cruel conquests of natives who fought desperately and to the point of death to defend their homes against the invaders. The months of marching and fighting had taken such heavy toll of both men and supplies that Belalcázar saw that he could not hope to push through to the high plains of the Chibchas in the one journey. He went back to Quito and gathered a new company, with more supplies, and came back to Popayán to start again. Now, as at last he neared his goal, he heard in his camp, as Quesada was hearing in Bogotá, of other Spaniards already on the ground. That was the worst news that could come to a conquistador, seeking for gold and lands to rule.

Belalcázar sent out scouts, and one of them, riding carelessly along beside a river's bank not far from the home camp, was startled to have his horse rear and refuse to go past a thicket of tall cane. The rider could see no danger, but the horse had smelled other horses

hidden there. The scout dashed back to camp, shouting loudly: "To arms! To arms! The enemy is here."

Seeing that they were discovered, the hidden party
came out. Hernán de Quesada had been sent by his
brother Gonzalo to find out about these "other white
men to the south." Twenty men rode out from cover
with their leader at their head and proceeded in the
direction from which the scout had come. Shortly they
were met by a company of Belalcázar's soldiers. The
two parties drew up opposite each other, while their
leaders saluted and exchanged explanations. Together
they rode back to the camp, where Belalcázar gave his
unwelcome guests tents but assigned guards to watch
them closely.

Now came one of those interviews between leaders
which remind us that these were all Spaniards, trained
in the same school of arms. Thousands of miles from
Europe, in a new and unexplored land, they carried
on their military relations with one another according
to the accepted standards of courtesy, even while they
applied no such rules to their dealings with the natives.

Hernán de Quesada recognized that the advantage
was on the side of this man whom he had ridden out to
find. These men from Quito were, as the Indian had
reported, in far better shape than his war-worn veterans.
They were equipped, as Spanish soldiers should be,

with fine armor and plumed helmets and cloth tunics. Their horses were fat and sleek from months spent in pleasant valleys. The Bogotá men were thin and browned by the sun so that they looked almost like the natives. They were dressed in worn, patched garments and rode on homemade skin saddles, which had taken the place of the leather ones worn out long since as they came up the Magdalena River.

Belalcázar saw these things, too, but he knew that the chief advantage was still on the side of the Quesadas. They had arrived first and were on the coveted ground. He accepted the invitation of Hernán de Quesada to come to Bogotá and visit his brother, wondering secretly how strong a force he would find in possession of this new province. Hernán de Quesada had offered such gifts as he had, some thin plates of gold and finely woven Indian cloths. Were these Quesadas concealing rich stores of gold and other treasure? Belalcázar wondered. But he did not speak his thought aloud. Instead he was generous in his return gifts and offered to loan horses and arms if they were needed for the further conquest of the Chibcha nation.

While the leaders were exchanging these courtesies, the common soldiers were more blunt with one another. Those on each side wanted to be sole owners of the land.

One of Quesada's captains heard the men arguing and said openly:

"Into these lands which we have won, no man shall enter, except at swords' point."

But another, overhearing, spoke more wisely.

"There is no need," he said, "of a decision by swords, for the cost of conquest of the natives has been too great. We have all won through to this place with much hardship. Far better that we Spaniards refrain from turning our swords against one another."

Belalcázar was of two minds whether or not to accept the invitation and continue his march to Bogotá. He had already taken a vast territory and established three towns. He was well supplied with arms, horses, and provisions. Should he continue on his independent way? He decided to delay while Hernán de Quesada went back to report to his brother, sending him off with gifts and saying only that he would probably follow soon.

But while Hernan had been away from Bogotá the strangest thing of all had happened—that which anyone would say could never happen. But it did!

III

To the armed camp at Bogotá, where Gonzalo de Quesada was anxiously awaiting his brother's return, there came another alarming message. It was a written word, traced with red ocher on a piece of polished deerskin. It came from a former member of his own expedition, a captain whom he had punished, because of his displeasure with him, by banishing him to a distant Indian village. He had not expected ever to hear of the man again. Such a sentence would probably mean death, for the natives were likely to turn on any single, unarmed Spaniard.

"Sir," the strange-appearing message read, "I have sure word that a band of Spaniards is near by. They are coming from the *llanos*. They will be here tomorrow. Let your worship decide quickly what he will do."

Gonzalo de Quesada was indeed in a tight place. The conquests which were so lately behind him had left him in bad shape for any more fighting. He had hardly any powder for his guns, and all his arms were in poor condition. No report had yet come from his brother as to how big a force of Spaniards was coming up from the south or whether the newcomers were disposed to be friendly or unfriendly. If two armies of any size should come down on him and his men at the same time, his proud claims of conquest of this rich land might prove to be as an idle breath, borne by the wind.

He was a man of action, of quick decision and courage; and he had his horses, those invaluable aids in the business of conquest. He ordered them saddled at once, and within a couple of hours of the coming of the message he set out with a mounted band of his most faithful men, whites and Indians, riding boldly in the direction from which these strangers were reported to be coming.

It was a brave-looking company that rode forth across the plain, and its leader gave no signs of the doubt which was in his mind. He passed through the village where the exiled captain had been living and added him to his force. So much, at least, the man had earned.

They rode on for many miles until they met—not an army, but a single rider, dressed in skins of animals, a thin, worn skeleton of a man with long hair and uncut beard, mounted on a hard-ridden, ill-fed horse. He drew up before Quesada and spoke in harsh, weary tones:

"I am Pedro Limpias, an old conquistador of Venezuela, and I come ahead of an expedition led by Captain Nicholas Federmann, and sent out by the governor of Venezuela, under the protection of His Majesty Emperor Charles V of Spain."

The men from Bogotá stared at him in utter astonishment. Why, Venezuela was on the seacoast, far to the east and north. The Chibchas had told them that between their nation and the tribes beyond the rivers and mountains there lay a land into which none of them had ever gone, for it was impassable. Yet here was this man who declared himself to be the scout for an expedition which had somehow won its way through.

With all eagerness an advance guard of Quesada's soldiers rode on, by his bidding, to succor such men as might be coming. When they met them these hardened veterans were moved almost to tears by their plight. Their leader, Captain Federmann, a man of German birth, reported that they had started three years before from Coro in Venezuela. A company of four hundred Spaniards, they had intended to explore the country, to find, if they could, El Dorado, which was, by their information, a city of enormous wealth and golden promise, and also to take possession of all lands which they might discover.

They had come from the seacoast to the foothills of the high mountains and then had taken what was said to be the better route across the continent, a way that led through the vast llanos. But these grassy plains proved to stretch out endlessly, like an ocean of grass, with rivers and marshes cutting through them. In the llanos Indians found them and attacked them, killing many of their number. Others died from disease or were drowned in the rivers and swamps. A man was lost forever if he got separated from his party or missed his path. The tropical rains came, and the clothes on their backs rotted and fell off. They replaced them with tunics made from the skins of animals which they caught, and bound their feet and legs with more skins. Yet the survivors pushed on, until at last they came to the edge of other mountains. Here they gained courage for their last hard march from tales which Indians in the foothills told them, tales of a land of treasure beyond the mountains, a House of the Sun filled with gold, El Dorado of their dreams.

Now they were here, the hundred who remained of the four hundred who had set out three years earlier. Somehow they had covered the last lap of the journey, pushing their way up the mountain trail and crossing on a path which overhung precipices, so that for the safety of their horses and mules they had to haul them along with ropes which they had made out of hemp. They had arrived, ragged, unkempt, hungry, but still with a few cocks and hens, which they had managed to bring with them all the long way on their horses' backs. They were ready to lay claim to this fair land which they had reached at such a price of suffering and toil.

When this story was brought back to him Quesada

knew that he must make a show of his power if he was
to prove his claim to the land. He sent forward Indian
cotton cloths, with which the newcomers might cover
themselves, and baskets of food for their comfort. Then
he summoned quickly as many Indians as he could from
the near-by villages. These he lined up in marching
order behind and beside his own soldiers. When Federmann and his men put in an appearance after their brief
rest, they were met by this large company. One of
Quesada's soldiers beat a march on his drum, and the
Indians blew loudly on their war pipes and into their
seashell horns.

Captain Federmann drew up his weary men in military order and then rode forward and was greeted by
Quesada. The two leaders embraced and rode back together over the plain to Bogotá, exchanging stories of
their experiences. Quesada found Federmann to be a
fine, honorable man, and the two came soon to an agreement to share the spoils of all future conquests, with
Quesada offering to the newcomers such extra equipment as he had.

IV

While these two companies were resting and feasting, up rode Belalcázar and his little army. He had
decided not to delay, but to come up and see for himself

this land to which he had been coming for so long a time. He, too, was welcomed, and he and his men were set up in a separate camp while the three leaders began to confer.

The Spanish chronicler Acosta gives the picture:

While the clergy and the religious were going to and fro from the different camps, endeavoring to prevent trouble, the three parties of Spaniards, coming from points so distant, and now occupying the three points of a triangle, whose sides measured three or four leagues [eight to ten miles], presented a singular spectacle. Those from Peru were clad in scarlet cloth and silk and wore steel helmets and costly plumes. Those from Santa Marta had cloaks, linens, and caps made by the Indians. Those, however, from Venezuela, like refugees from Robinson Crusoe's island, were covered with the skins of bears, leopards, tigers, and deer.

Fortunately all three leaders had sense enough to see that no good would come of quarreling with one another. Under the skillful leadership of Quesada, the lawyer-conqueror, they came to an agreement as to the division of their conquests. On the advice of Belalcázar, who had had experience in colonizing, Quesada set about improving his capital, laying out a more ambitious town with brick houses instead of huts of wood with straw roofs. Quesada and Federmann had already made their terms as to future conquests. Belalcázar, after looking over the ground, declared himself satisfied with the great territory to the south which he had already occupied. Dreams of El Dorado still haunted them all, but the picture was changed now from that of a Gilded Man to that of a golden city, a House of the Sun filled with gold. Being practical gentlemen, they decided that they must return at once to Spain and establish at court their claims to the territory they had already taken, before they did more exploration.

The three conquistadors lived together on the plain of Bogotá while a ship was being built at a port on the Magdalena River to take them home to Spain. At last they departed together, intending to present their story at court, where they should receive from the emperor suitable rewards for their discoveries in the way of territorial rights and high governing officers.

As so often happened in the case of the conquistadors, they did not receive such rewards. Each one of these men had carried through an exploring expedition of the first rank. They had gone through terrific hardships. But the control of the regions of which they brought the first information was handed over by the emperor to court favorites, officials to be sent out newly from Spain.

To Quesada, Belalcázar, and Federmann remained, however, their lasting claims to fame. They had taken an important part in the opening up of the New World. The whole northern area of the new continent, discovered only some thirty-five years earlier, was now known. Colonists and other explorers were soon to follow in their wake. Quesada had founded Bogotá, which was to be one of the leading cities of South America. He returned to it a few years later, and his remains repose today in its cathedral.

South America has always been a land of treasure. The first explorers went back to Spain exhibiting ornaments of solid gold and casting around pearls "as if they were chaff," as one chronicler has put it. She is still a land of treasure, with her riches tempting explorers in every decade. Today her riverbanks are being searched for orchids and medicinal herbs; her mountains, for tin, copper, and coal; her forests, for rubber and mahogany; and her inland plateaus, for deposits of oil, the "black gold" of the twentieth century. In all the world's history no search for treasure is so amazing as the century-long quest for El Dorado. In that quest these three conquistadors staged one of the strangest meetings in all history. To their everlasting credit, they made peace with one another instead of disputing one another's claims and fighting to maintain their rights.

Father Fritz
Maps the Amazon

"I WENT WITHOUT PAUSE BY DAY OR
NIGHT UP AND DOWN THE GREAT RIVER."

Samuel Fritz

ON THE STREETS OF THE LUXURY-
loving Spanish city of Lima, Peru, there appeared one
day in the year 1692 a strange figure: a priest, tall, thin,
with ruddy countenance and long, curly beard. He was
wearing a short cassock of palm fiber instead of the
usual cloth robe, with hempen sandals on his feet and
a cross of chonta wood in his hand. With him walked
several Indians, tall, fine-looking men, but of strange

face and dress, different from the natives of the Peruvian capital.

It was as if in the days of the New Testament John the Baptist had suddenly appeared from the wilderness in his garment of camel's hair on the fashionable streets of Rome or Alexandria. The people ran together from all parts of the city to see the sight, but while they gazed curiously, there was no one who did not know from the mere sight of Father Fritz that he was a holy man. They conducted him to the establishment of the Jesuits, and there the members of his own order received him warmly, and his Indians with him. There he waited until an audience with the viceroy could be arranged.

Until our own century Father Samuel Fritz, Jesuit missionary in South America at the end of the seventeenth century and the beginning of the eighteenth, was known chiefly by his map of the Amazon River. During the forty years of his service as "Apostle to the Indians," he drew and redrew this map of the Amazon region which was to be used by explorers who followed him. It is no such map as used to appear in the old school geographies and in medieval wonder books, with wild beasts and picturesque Indians drawn in to fill spaces which would otherwise have been marked unknown. This is an amazing, detailed, intricate drawing, which looks like a picture of the blood stream of the human body, with hundreds of arteries and veins running out from a central trunk. Most of these lines, and the spaces between them, are labeled with names—strange, unfamiliar Indian names—and each of those wavy lines, so carefully sketched in, stands for a river or stream which Father Fritz saw with his own eyes. The distances between the rivers and streams that are shown as flowing into the main current of the Upper Amazon are measured or calculated. The heights of the falls have been taken and the levels of the waters recorded. Father Fritz was not given to extolling his own work. His hardships during his long missionary work are passed over lightly in his journal. But on the map is written in his own hand the statement that he has made it "with no little toil and exertion, having navigated the river in the greater part of its course as far as it is navigable."

Until a few years ago this map and a few references to Father Fritz in contemporary letters and histories were all that were known of this explorer-missionary. But early in this twentieth century a long-lost manuscript, with portions of his own journal and a brief account of his life written by an intimate friend, was discovered in a Portuguese library.

Samuel Fritz was a native of Bohemia, born in 1654, a student who showed such intellectual brilliance during his years in the Jesuit college that his superiors in the order had marked him as one who would advance to high positions. But after a few years of university life he turned his back on these tempting prospects and chose the vocation of missionary, coming in 1686 to faraway Quito, now the capital of Ecuador, then a part of Peru, on the west coast of South America.

If he had stayed in Quito or gone south to Lima, where there were several Jesuit establishments, his life would not have differed very greatly from that which he had left behind. In Lima there were a university, a cathedral, and many churches. But it was to be six years before Father Fritz was to make his dramatic entry into Lima, and in the year of his arrival he did not expect ever to visit that city. The young missionary put behind him the opportunity for a comfortable life of teaching and elected to go out into the wilderness. He chose to make the difficult journey across the great mountain wall of the Andes and search out the wild Indian tribes of the river forests.

Others had made that choice before him, and the story of their endeavors, as Father Fritz was told it at Quito, was such as to give even a brave man pause. Nearly one hundred and fifty years before, Gonzalo Pizarro and Orellana had crossed the mountain wall and explored the Amazon in search of treasure, Orellana making the spectacular journey to the river's mouth which brought him out on the Atlantic, with the first west-to-east crossing of the continent at this wide point to his credit. Since those days solitary priests had sallied forth with their wooden crosses, seeking to carry the gospel to the river tribes. Often they did not return, and no one knew whether they lost their lives through accident or illness or met death at the hands of the savages.

Early in the seventeenth century the government had attempted to establish settlements and forts in one Amazon region, but the soldiers treated the natives with such cruelty that they rebelled, attacking the forts and then fleeing to the safety of the trackless woods to escape punishment. It was then that the soldier-governor turned to the church. There was little hope, he reported, of conquering the wild peoples by force, but the missionaries might succeed in "tranquilizing them by persuasion."

Two Jesuit fathers responded to the call. One of them, on his arrival, asked the chief of an important Indian tribe how many nations there were in these forests. The chief took up a handful of sand and tossed it to the winds.

"Countless as the grains of sand are the nations in this land," he said; "for there is neither lake nor river, hill nor valley, plain nor forest, which is not full of inhabitants."

That was fifty years before the coming of Father Fritz, and the thirty tiny mission stations which had been established during that time were almost as scattered and lost as the chief's grains of sand, in the vast region to which he was electing to go.

Father Fritz went alone and carried on most of his early work alone, save for the company of the "dear children," his natives whom he soon gathered around him. To them this tall, redheaded, kindly man was a miracle, sent straight from that heaven of which he told, to deliver them from their fears of evil spirits and nature gods and from their many misfortunes and diseases.

"I went without pause by day or night up and down the great river," he said of himself.

He carried in his canoe only his wooden cross, his small portable altar, and his bell to give the call to worship. The people came in crowds to listen to his preaching and were persuaded to gather in villages and learn the civilizing ways of the new faith. They brought their sick to him, and he did what he could for them, drawing on such medical knowledge as he possessed and a kindly wisdom about the laws of health.

It was not an easy miracle that he performed. There were those in every tribe who worked against him. He knew well that at any moment these "children of the forest," who looked on him as almost a divine being, might turn against him for some unknown cause or in anger at some simple word of reproof and put him out in the wilderness alone to die.

In the third year of his ministry he was taken desperately ill, with a swelling of the limbs and a fever, so that he was in constant severe pain and too weak to move himself. He was at the village of the Jurimaguas when this heavy sickness came upon him, and in that month the annual flood of the river brought the waters to such an extraordinary height that the whole village was almost covered. Most of the people fled to the forests, but the few who remained cared for him. He was moved to a shelter on the roof of one of the houses and lay there for three months, "only a handbreadth," as he wrote, "above the rushing flood." There he lay, sleepless from pain, although he might not have been able to sleep otherwise with the gruntings of the alligators and crocodiles and lizards beneath him. His devoted Indians brought him such small supplies of food as they could get, but the rats came and fed on it, becoming so bold that they gnawed his spoon and plate and the handle of his knife.

There came a day when he knew that he could stay no longer, unless it were to meet his death. He must get down the river to some place where he could receive medical aid. "More dead than alive," as he says, he was carried down the river in a canoe, into Portuguese territory, stopping first at a Christian mission station where he was kindly cared for and then being taken, because of the seriousness of his illness, to the city of Pará, just inland from the Atlantic Ocean. Though he was so ill, he gathered much information on the way down the river for his map. He was always observing, recording, and sketching for his future use.

At Pará, Father Fritz recovered his health but met other trouble. The governments of Spain and Portugal were disputing over the possession of the Upper Amazon basin. In the region where he had been laboring there were said to be markers, set up by a Portuguese explorer a half century earlier. Since Father Fritz came from the Spanish city of Quito, he was considered a Spanish disturber of the peace, who might make trouble among the Indians for the Portuguese traders as they came up the river claiming these villages.

Suspected of being a spy, he was detained in Pará for twenty-two months, until finally orders came directly from the king in Portugal ordering his release and instructing the Brazilian officials to conduct him up the river to his mission. On this return journey he made great progress with his map, laying out the river's course and marking the streams which entered it.

It was a sad journey, however, and a sad return.

Portuguese traders were entering all the villages, exchanging implements of iron, glass beads, and cheap manufactured articles for the sarsaparilla, balsam, gums, resins, and wax which the Indians had to offer. But such trading was only a beginning. The Portuguese carried off men, women, and children to be sold on the coast as slaves. They were planning to do so in his own region as soon as they had delivered him to his forest home. But when he came to that home other traders had been there before them. The villages were emptied or destroyed and the mission houses gone. The natives had fled before the white men's raids and the destruction caused by a severe earthquake.

When the news of the holy father's safe return spread, his people came out from their jungle homes to greet him with rejoicing. If he had been there, they told him, the earthquake would not have happened. It was a punishment sent by his God because of the wickedness of the Portuguese in imprisoning him. They carried him ashore from his canoe to the center of their new village, celebrating the event with feasting and dancing to the music of drums, fifes, and wood flutes. It is one of the happy pictures of the good father's life, this finding of his people in their forests, after he had thought them all dead or enslaved, and being welcomed by them as one returned from the dead.

Father Fritz stayed for a year on the rivers, but the raids continued. He made up his mind that the Spanish authorities in Peru must know what was being done. This boundary dispute was a matter between two nations. He left his mission station and set out for Lima, going by a new, unexplored river route and marking its course on his precious map as he went.

One wonders if this simple priest, who had come to Quito from Bohemia and never set foot in Spain, had any notion of the place to which he was coming. Lima, Pizarro's "City of Kings," rivaled in gaiety and luxury the finest cities in Europe. A new viceroy had come recently, Melchor Portocarrero, Count of Montclova, a distinguished military officer who had held a like position in Mexico. The city had been recovering, when he arrived, from the destructive earthquake of 1687. The first task of the new viceroy had been to help the citizens, by grants of government money, in the rebuilding of their beautiful city.

Here, on that day in 1692, appeared Father Fritz in his fiber cassock, with hempen sandals on his feet and Indians of an unfamiliar tribe escorting him. It was as if he came from another world, as indeed he did, a world of savage life within the jungle. The members of the Jesuit Order who took him in arranged an audience with the viceroy, and he declared that he was going to it just as he was, in his own ragged fiber cassock. Only when they represented to him that he must wear a cloth cassock for the honor of the order, and to show proper respect at court, did he reluctantly yield.

So the two worlds came together, the world of Father Fritz and the world of the viceroy, a man who enjoyed the pomp and luxury that went with his office and seldom went outside his palace except in his carriage with its six horses and an escort of outriders.

To the eternal honor of the Count of Montclova be it remembered that he received the holy man with the utmost love and veneration. There were many interviews after that first one. The viceroy sent almost daily for Father Fritz and sat with him for hours, questioning him and listening while he told of the customs of the jungle and river people, of the conversions he had made to Christianity, and of the strange country on either side of the river. The father told, too, of the way the Portuguese were claiming territory which he thought belonged to Spain and of their cruel treatment of his "children." The traders had so many gifts for them, things which the simple folk coveted, the gay-colored cloths, and the beads, and other trifles; and he, the missionary, had none. That, at least, could be remedied, the viceroy said. He himself would see that the holy man was well supplied with such articles to carry back as gifts and for barter.

The viceroy would have kept Father Fritz in Lima, but as soon as he felt that his errand was done he declared that he must return to his work. Before he left he drew maps of the region such as no one else could have drawn, maps which showed what lands belonged to Spain and were being taken away from her. The viceroy had the whole story written down and promised to send it to the king. When Father Fritz and his Indians started on the long journey back, he had all the gold and silver which the viceroy could make him take, money drawn from his own private store, not from the government treasury. As the holy father and his six Indians made their way back they took the heights of the rivers and waterfalls at every stopping place along the new route. Father Fritz never forgot the map he was drawing.

During the next twenty years the missionary founded at least forty villages among the Amazon River tribes, bringing the people together out of their wild, wandering life. He helped the people to build churches in them, for he could be a good carpenter when the need arose. He was an artist, too, and made sacred paintings for their altars, pictures which were found many years after his death. Sharing the people's daily life, he did not hesitate to share their dangers. There is a record in his journal of an attack made upon the tribe with which he was living by a heathen people from a distance. Hearing the disturbance, he hurried to the scene.

"I ran up with my Cross," he writes, "to die with or for my converts."

The trouble which he foretold came upon his people. What he was building, other white men tore down. His "children" had to leave their villages and move farther and farther away from the river in order to escape the traders and slave catchers. For the last ten years of his life he had to leave them and go to work among another Indian people, a warlike nation dwelling safely on streams farther from the Amazon. There he lived until his death in 1724, when he was within a month of his seventieth birthday.

He stands as a conspicuous example of the double work done by devoted church fathers, that of civilizing the people and of opening up unknown regions. But the place to look for Father Samuel Fritz's name is not in church records, though it might be found there. It is in the list of South America's early scientists. The map which he made with "no little toil and exertion" admits him to that company as a geographer of no mean skill and learning.

The Horse
Comes to South America

"FOR, AFTER GOD, WE OWED THE VICTORY
TO THE HORSES."—*A Conquistador*

IF THE INCAS AND CHIBCHAS AND OTHER
native peoples of South America had been telling of
their conquest by these white men, every story
would have begun with a tale of the strange, tall beasts
which seemed almost to be a part of the conquerors.
One of the bravest acts of the unhappy Inca emperor
Atahualpa, from whom Pizarro took Peru, was at that
first meeting of the two leaders in the great square of

Caxamarca, when the royal Indian gave no start of surprise or fear when one of these amazing giant creatures snorted in his face.

At first the Indians thought that the gunfire which blazed from their riders was from the horses' nostrils, while the sound of the guns' report was their bellowing. Pizarro's twenty-seven horses, which he had brought overseas and up by steep mountain passes to Peru, did as much in the conquest as his less than two hundred men. The shrewd Spanish conquistadors came to consider a horse worth any ten or twelve men in a campaign against native tribes, and there were those who said that they would reckon a single horse as worth one hundred men.

The Spaniards had been horsemen at home and cared for their thoroughbred steeds as a knight of old cared for his mount. The chroniclers list the horses' names, one by one, and give their color and breed. They tell of the help each horse gave on an expedition, as if it were a person, and grieve over the death of a favorite steed. They did well to give this credit, for the horses must carry them safely over the mountain passes and swim with them on their backs across the rivers; and the strong, willing, intelligent animals did not fail them.

The horses were protected on jungle trips with a special cotton "armor," an *escaupile,* such as the soldiers

themselves wore. On the trip of Quesada up the Magdalena River, from the Caribbean coast to the plain of
Bogotá, he and his men were constantly harassed by
Indians lurking along the riverbanks and in the jungles,
who shot poisoned arrows at them. The usual armor,
brought from Spain, was not sure to turn these weapons
back, but the ingenious explorers devised a heavy cotton
quilting, "three fingers thick," which did the trick.
They made coats and helmets for themselves and then
provided them for their horses, giving each a head-
piece and a blanket cover which reached from back
to hoof. The animals were, as a chronicler writes, a
"monstrous sight" when they were so arrayed; but the
arrows stuck fast in the padding instead of going
through it. At night it was the soldiers' task to pull the
arrows from the horses' armor before they took it off
them. Often there would be eight or ten or even a
dozen arrows embedded in each *escaupile*.

The horses became more than conquerors or helpers
of their conquering masters. They started their own
"colonies," too, if one may use that word, and why not?
A colony is, according to the dictionary, a "company
. . . transplanted from their mother country to a remote
land" or "sojourning in a foreign land." Would not the
horses have so described themselves, if they could have
done so? They came to a land where the only animals

which resembled them were the llamas, three feet or so high, called by the Spaniards "little camels" because of their long necks, the beasts of burden of the Andes mountain tribes, and there they "sojourned."

We can even follow the beginnings of one of these horse "colonies." When the news of Pizarro's rich finds in Peru was brought to Spain, there were many adventurers who were eager to come out to the New World in the hope of discovering another empire like that of the wealthy Incas. One of these persons was a rich Basque gentleman, Pedro de Mendoza, who sought to colonize the Plata region on the southeast coast of South America. That part of the continent had had a tragic history for explorers. Spanish exploration of the east coast had begun with Vicente Pinzón, who had commanded the *Niña* on Columbus' first voyage. He and a companion, Juan Díaz de Solís, one of the foremost navigators of the time, had made a second trip, sailing around Brazil and probably as far south as the present Uruguay. Solís had come out again, five years before Magellan's epochal voyage, with orders from King Ferdinand to explore the southern lands and find a strait through to Balboa's "South Sea" and the Orient. Going inland on the wide Plata estuary, where the cities of Montevideo and Buenos Aires now stand, he had been killed by Indians. The Spaniards were to learn to their sorrow that the savage, warlike tribes of these regions were very different from the more civilized and peaceful Incas and Chibchas on the western side of the continent.

Ten years later Sebastian Cabot had come out to investigate this same river and hopefully named it Rio de la Plata (river of silver), although there was no silver, thus giving the present name of Argentina (silver land) to the great southern stretch of land. He failed to make a successful settlement, and to bring out precious metals, because of the hostility of the Indians. Returning to Spain, he told, however, of an amazing land, with the pampas, vast treeless plains stretching as far as the eye could see, covered with a sea of grass taller than a man's head as he stood in it.

No such tale failed to find its hearers in those days of gallant adventure. Don Pedro de Mendoza, officer of the household of Emperor Charles V, a soldier of repute, made an arrangement with the emperor to colonize the region. All the expenses of the expedition were to be his, and for his part he agreed to take with him

> 1000 men,
> 100 horses and mares,

8 "religious," or priests,
1 doctor,
1 apothecary,
1 surgeon.

He was to build three forts for the protection of the colony and to seek out a land route to Peru, which had come to be recognized as the chief source of gold and treasure.

Nobles and gentlemen flocked to Seville, seeking to be included in the number permitted to go. When the fourteen ships sailed in 1535 there were twenty-five hundred people aboard, counting the sailors as well as the families of the colonists and the thousand soldiers. The lordly gentlemen and ladies would have been amazed to know that the chief contribution of that grand expedition was to be the horses and mares which were to be left behind by its survivors.

The value of the horses was first recognized at the time of landing. It had been a hard trip across the waters. Mendoza had been ill all the way. The people were in miserable condition, as provisions had run short, and the horses, on which all conquest depended, were weak and sick. The first man to land was Mendoza's brother-in-law. Coming from the crowded, ill-smelling cabins below decks, he caught the smell of the fresh, life-giving air which blew in from the pampas and made his famous comment on "buenos aires," giving the future city its name. But the lords and ladies were not to be the first to step on land and breathe deeply of those "good airs," though everyone must have been eager to come ashore after the weary weeks aboard ship. The horses were landed first. They must be cared for at all odds, even if human beings had to wait.

These men were ill suited to the hard work of colonizing. They did not know enough to sow a crop before winter came, though they were ready to fight the Indians bravely when the first attacks came. Twenty-five of the precious horses were lost in battle in the first expedition inland against the Indians, and the men mourned them as they did their fallen comrades at arms. On that march the Spaniards saw the grassy, treeless pampas, on which bands of ostriches and packs of deer were running, but never a horse. The expedition was unlucky from the start. Parties went inland and finally succeeded in founding small settlements which survived. But Mendoza's fortified town, Santa Maria de los Buenos Aires, could not survive. Its inhabitants, threatened by famine, disease, and hostile natives, were forced to abandon it. Of the twenty-five hundred who had come out from Spain, there were left in the whole Plata region within a year less than six hundred survivors. Some of these stayed on in the inland forts, but the rest, with their sick leader, Mendoza, sailed sadly back to Spain.

They left, however, probably without intention and for lack of space on the ships, *seven horses and five mares*. That was the beginning of the independent "colony" of horses which was to grow into a great "nation," spreading far over the pampas.

The climate and conditions were perfect for these animals, left to fend for themselves after a lifetime of being cared for by the masters whom they served. There were grassy plains, with streams and pools everywhere to furnish them with water. The temperature was never too severe for their comfort, and there were few wild animals that would attack them. Moreover, the fierce Indians, who were perfectly willing to attack armed soldiers, were in great terror of these strange, tall animals. There is a story that when one of the Spanish parties went inland to explore, the Indians begged the governor to "speak to the horses and ask them not to be angry, and tell them that food would be brought to them."

Spaniards were finding it difficult to take possession of this land, but the horses adopted it as their own. A trained horse, brought out from Spain, was for many years a most precious possession to the soldier-settlers. Such a horse was sold for four thousand golden crowns in 1551 in Paraguay, in an exchange between two officers. But scores of half-wild horses were running the plains. Soon the Indians lost their fear of these animals which shared the pampas with them. They caught and rode them, using no stirrups but only a halter made of reeds or skin.

The horse was to change the life of the Indian. Tribes which had stayed in one region were to go farther afield. As they wandered over greater reaches of territory, the mounted Indians became more difficult to attack and conquer.

The white men, too, the Spaniards who remained to colonize, were to be changed by the character of the land and of the horses bred on it. The first comers had had to live in villages, as our North American colonists of the seacoasts did. But soon men from the Plata villages were to go out singly and in pairs and make their homes on the plains. Many of them married Indian wives, and from these homes came the Gauchos of the Argentine plains, who were to have so large a part in shaping the destiny of the country.

The first horses "settled" on the pampas between 1536 and 1550. In 1774 an Englishman, Father Falkner, describes wild horses as the chief "inhabitants" of the plains. When he and four Indians went on an inland trip they were likely, as they journeyed, to be caught in the midst of herds of wild horses which took two and three hours to pass. The animals moved in such close formation that the members of the little party feared lest they be trampled to death by them.

In those days, if a man wanted to tame a troop of horses, he had only to catch them, one by one, by lasso and train them. Father Falkner tells that there were so many tamed horses on the ranches or in the towns that he could have bought a two-year-old colt for half a dollar and a full-grown horse for two dollars. Cattle also abounded, and any man, whether Spaniard, half-breed, or Indian, could make his living by means of his knife or his lasso. If he wanted money, he could sell hides. There was no need for him to cultivate the soil or make a permanent home.

Such a life made for a passion for independence. When Bolívar and San Martín called for volunteers to aid them in throwing off the yoke of Spain and freeing South America, the men of the pampas of Argentina and the llanos of Venezuela responded. These treeless plains of the Orinoco basin in the north were different from the southern pampas. On the llanos life was more difficult for horses and cattle because of the tropical character of the country. Floods were matched by frequent droughts. Waters were infested with crocodiles, and there were all sorts of animal life to plague the creatures, from swarms of insects to sting their hides and suck their blood to marauding tigers to pounce upon them and kill them.

Such conditions breed strong animals and strong men. Here Bolívar, the Liberator, found one of his most valuable leaders in the fight for independence in the first part of the nineteenth century. The story of Páez, the *llanero* chief, and of his taking of enemy steamboats by his troop of horsemen is known to every schoolboy in South America.

José Antonio Páez had grown up on the llanos. As a boy he had fled from his native town on the edge of the plains, because of a murder committed in self-defense, and hidden himself on a cattle ranch. Herds of cattle roamed the llanos, with boys and men on horseback to watch over them. Páez won a hard-earned leadership among his fellow llaneros by the time he was twenty-one. When the fight with the Spaniards began, many of these men left their cattle herding and joined the armies, some on one side, some on the other, in the great struggle. When Páez decided to throw in his lot with the rebels, most of his followers went with him.

General Bolívar, coming up the Orinoco River to the region where the llaneros were waging an independent war and winning victories, invited the wild young chieftain to come to meet him. The two came to an agreement. There was that quality of leadership in Bolívar which brought such men to his side. Combining their forces, the two marched to a place where their progress was halted by the sight of armed ships of the Spaniards anchored midstream on the river. Bolívar was waiting for his own boats, due to come up the river from the coast, but they were delayed. The days of waiting lengthened beyond the patience of the llanero chieftain.

"Why are we waiting?" he asked Bolívar, knowing well the answer that would come.

"For boats to carry our troops farther up the river," replied the Liberator.

"Let us take the boats of the Spaniards," said Páez shortly.

"How shall we take them?" asked Bolívar.

"With our cavalry," said Páez, and prepared to do so before Bolívar's astonished eyes.

The llanero chieftain led fifty of his trained horsemen to the river's bank. At his word they dashed into the stream, keeping up a constant shouting to frighten away the alligators. The tumult and surprise made the Spaniards think that they were being attacked by a great army. Reaching the vessels, the llaneros leaped from their horses' backs and swarmed over the sides, while the Spaniards took to their canoes in all haste and fled to the opposite bank of the river. The boats were taken for Bolívar. A fleet taken by cavalry, for the only time in the history of the Americas! The horse had won a place on the roll of honor of South America.

Dyewood
and Diamonds in Brazil

DISCOVERY ALMOST BY ACCIDENT

A LITTLE FLEET OF PORTUGUESE SHIPS,
bound for the East Indies by the route around Africa,
touched South America, in the year 1500, on the bulging coast of Brazil. The commander, Pedro Cabral, did
a little exploring but could not stop long to investigate
this land which he thought to be a large island. He must
be on his way to the Orient, but he took the precaution
of claiming the land in the name of King Manuel of

Portugal and sending one of his ships back with news of the find and a cargo of a dyewood discovered ashore, a wood like the *brasil* wood known in Europe.

From this wood Brazil got its name; but a colony without gold created little or no excitement in Portugal. Men came out in their ships, during the next fifty or one hundred years, to get loads of this and other woods. Settlers took possession of some of the rich plantation lands. But the picture of the new land was fixed in people's minds. It was a land without gold, destined to be a colony with forest products and for the raising of stock. Sugar cane could be cultivated there. The early comers laid the foundation for the great sugar crops of later days. But Brazil went along without any special advertising.

In 1693 the gold rush began, but it started slowly, without giving promise of what was to come. Small quantities of gold were found in the south, but the king had to offer rewards to make the people go out and search for more. Then the rush was on. Rich deposits of gold were located. Brazil had its El Dorado in the "Great Mines," Minas Geraes, as the province where they were located was named. Gold changed the country and the inhabitants. There had been, from the early days of discovery and exploration, a growing race of adventurers in these regions, half-breeds from the mating of Portuguese settlers and Indians. Flag-bearers, *bandeirantes*, they were called, as they went up the rivers, through the forests, into the interior, always on the hunt for gold and slaves, always taking new lands.

Now, when the gold had been discovered in the river beds, there poured in fortune hunters from Portugal and from the sugar plantations and settled regions to the north. The flag-bearers were pushed back and went into the wilderness, seeking and finding more mines. For thirty years gold poured in a steady stream across the seas to Portugal.

Then, as the mines began to be worked out, another discovery was made. The first discovery was by accident; the second, in another region, was hardly more expected.

On a mountain range Negro laborers, digging for gold, picked up shining pebbles, noticeable for their regular geometrical shapes, and put them in their pockets. They were fond of playing cards and used the stones as counters, to keep the record of their games. A man happened along who had lived in the East Indies. He noticed the pile of pebbles and thought them diamonds. He tested them by weight, comparing them with other pebbles of the same weight, and found them heavier. Men in Lisbon and jewelers in Holland tested samples sent overseas and pronounced them diamonds of rare size and value. The search for more such pebbles began.

In another region a similar discovery was made. Three men were convicted of crimes in a Brazilian court and sent into the wilderness for lifelong exile. Their names are remembered all down the years, not for the crimes they committed, but for the discovery which they made. They were Antonio de Sousa, José Felix Gómaz, and Tomás de Sousa. These men were forbidden to enter any city or town or hold any communication with the world. It was a living death, which might end at any moment in actual death from the dangers of the jungle.

Yet men are so made up that they never accept the worst. Antonio, José, and Tomás began, as the months went by, to follow their old ways and search in the river beds for glittering grains of gold. If only they could find a little gold, they might by some means manage to exchange it for some of the things they needed to make themselves more comfortable.

One day during the dry season, as they were washing for gold in a shallow river, they came upon a stone which looked to them like a large diamond. Here was something better than they could have hoped for, but of what good was it to them? There was a law against washing for gold, and they had been breaking it. Then, they were forbidden to talk with anyone or to enter a town. Yet what if this was a diamond, as they were quite sure it was? At last an idea came to them. No one, not even a judge, could forbid anyone's talking with a priest. That was a right above any law.

They went together to the nearest priest, a man who had been kind to them when they were on their way into the wilderness, and showed him the gem. With no thought of the punishment which might be his for dealing with these outlawed men, he brought them to a spot near the town where the governor of Minas Geraes lived. Here he left them hidden, bidding them to wait while he went and showed the gem. It was tested and pronounced to be of great value.

The priest had said only that it had been found. Now he told the story of how he had come by it.

"I want you to pardon these men," he said, and the governor agreed that he should do so. But the law was the law. Only the king was above it. The sentence had been passed, and only the king could take it back.

The stone was sent across the ocean to the king of Portugal and up to Holland to be tested by a jeweler there. In Minas Geraes and in Lisbon the men who examined it had been sure, but the word of an expert was desired. The report came back that this was a diamond of unusually fine quality and size. It had been found in a region where no search had ever been made. So its value as a stone, though great, was as nothing compared to its importance. This might be, as it proved to be, the sign of a rich diamond field. The king confirmed the pardon of the discoverers and set them free. The kindly priest was also rewarded.

These discoveries took place in the early part of the eighteenth century, from 1728 on. Brazil became the leading diamond center of the world and remained so for one hundred and fifty years, until the discovery of the Kimberley mines in South Africa in 1870. In the first hundred years twenty million dollars' worth of gems were shipped out of the country to the world's markets. But it was not the diamonds that counted most in Brazil's history, but rather the people whom they drew to the country.

As in our own California, with its gold rush, many of the immigrants who came for the mines stayed on to settle the lands, turning to ranching and farming. Others went exploring in the Amazon basin and down into Paraguay. They were a hardy, rough group of men who cared nothing for boundaries between Portuguese and Spanish lands as they had been drawn on the maps of the kings in Europe two hundred years before. Singly and in companies they pushed on, up the rivers, over the hills, through the jungles, marrying native women, breeding a new, strong race. The boundaries of Portuguese Brazil were being extended far across the continent. Spain did not like it, but in that far wilderness what could be done?

Meanwhile the work at the diamond mines went on, but such labor was not for adventurous, freeborn men. Negro slaves had been brought into Brazil in great numbers to do the work which the Portuguese planters and owners required on sugar plantations and in the gold mines. An Englishman by the name of John Mawe, author of books on precious stones, visited the country in 1804 and published, shortly after, a book on his "Travels in the Interior of Brazil, Particularly in the Gold and Diamond Districts." He gives a picture of the mines in Mandanoa, far in the interior, reached by a difficult journey, yet the scene of great activity. Here he found the officials, who were in charge of the mine, living in real elegance in spite of the wild surroundings. Excellent meals were served him in their homes, served on fine Wedgwood china sent over from England. But his interest was in the diamond works.

There was a river here, the bed of which had been found to be rich in diamonds. At this particular time the owners were working a bend or elbow in this wide river. A canal had been built above this bend, to carry off the water, and a dam made by piling up several thousand bags of sand. The river bed was then made dry by chain pumps, worked by a water wheel. It was an amazing engineering undertaking for such a wilderness.

From the river bed were next taken up cartloads of mud and gravel, which were carried to a long shed with troughs, on either side of which the Negroes worked, searching the dirt, as it passed them, for diamonds. Three overseers sat on high seats, overlooking the work. When a Negro found a stone he stood upright, clapped his hands, and then stretched his arm out, holding the gem between his forefinger and his thumb.

The Negroes were supplied by their owners and got, for this laborious work, about fifteen cents a day. But there was always before them the possibility of a rich reward. For stones of any value there was some slight extra pay. But for the larger ones, those weighing eight or ten carats, there was the prize of a new outfit, consisting of two new shirts, a suit, a hat, and a handsome knife. These heavier stones were found just often enough to keep the men on the alert. Then there was the highest possible reward, a man's freedom. That came for one who had the good fortune to find a 17½ carat stone, a very large gem and one of great value. The finder of such a stone was crowned with a wreath

of flowers and carried to the administrator, who summoned his owner and paid for him, then gave him his
freedom for life, with a present of new clothes thrown
in for good measure. While Mr. Mawe was there a
very large stone was found, and owners and officials
watched while it was found to be only 16½ carats in
weight, all showing, as the Englishman remarks, real
sympathy for the disappointed Negro who lost his
freedom by so narrow a margin.

It is a picture of the past, of more than a century ago.
Yet it was by such discoveries of treasure that South
America was opened up. In these years a race of Americans was coming into being. Wealth was being drawn
from the country, but some of it was remaining, and
the men who made it were building rich cities. In
Europe old fights were being fought. While Negroes
searched the gravel of Mandanoa for diamonds, the
kings who spent the wealth thus gained were being
pushed off their thrones by Napoleon Bonaparte. When
the chance came, the Brazilian people were to be eager
for freedom from overseas control. They had won this
land and worked it. They knew that it was theirs.

A Frenchman
Experiments with Rubber

CHARLES DE LA CONDAMINE VISITS THE
EQUATOR IN 1736

IN A PUBLIC SQUARE IN QUITO, ECUADOR,
there stands today a monument to three French scientists who came to that "equator capital" two hundred
years ago and spent seven years in making a world-
famous measurement of great scientific value. Not that
they stayed long in the comfortable Spanish city of
Quito! Far from it! That city was the headquarters
from which they went out into the high valleys and

up the sides of the lofty mountains which surround the plateau, nine or ten thousand feet above sea level, where Incas and Spaniards had built their homes.

There are many reasons why men undertake journeys of exploration into unknown lands. Underneath there is always a love of adventure, a spirit which drives them out of the easy, familiar comfort of their lives to battle against unknown odds. The conquistadors of Spain came to South America in the sixteenth century with two purposes: to find wealth for themselves and their king, and to extend the Christian faith among the natives who dwelt in these parts. But along with the lure of gold there was also the lure of the unknown. From the beginning of time men have always had a great curiosity about the world in which they lived. That curiosity, that passion for knowledge, is responsible for as much adventurous exploration as any El Dorado.

Sir Isaac Newton was the man who really gave the start to this scientific expedition to South America, though he never knew it, having died a few years before it was undertaken. In the course of elaborate figuring, in connection with his theory of gravitation, he raised a question. The shape of the earth, he believed, was not that of a round ball, but of a sphere, somewhat flattened and leveled at the poles and bulging at the equator. What did it matter? Ask any scientist of that day or this. On such knowledge depended the accuracy of future maps and navigation charts, the figuring of tables giving the position of the stars, and other information which all scientists desired.

There was one way to find out, and only one. Men must go as near the poles as they could, and to the equator, and take measurements. With no hesitation the newly organized French Academy of Science decided that this should be done. That such expeditions would be expensive, difficult, and dangerous mattered not at all. They must be made. The Academy called for volunteer scientists, as Peary and Byrd have called, in our day, for volunteers, and then chose the best men from the fairly large number of those who wanted to go.

Charles Marie de la Condamine, a mathematician and a seasoned explorer, was one of the first chosen. He had already made several Mediterranean voyages, exploring along the coasts of Africa and Asia and writing up his experiences for publication. Two expeditions were going, one to Lapland, which was as near the North Pole as it was possible to get, and the other to some spot on the equator. The choice here lay between Africa and South America. Peru (which then included Ecuador) was selected because there were Spanish cities there, with schools and colleges on which to draw for help, while the interior of Africa was almost entirely unknown. Condamine was to be one of the three leading men, with two fellow scientists from the French Academy as companions. The party included a surgeon, an engineer from the French navy, an instrument maker to care for the scientific apparatus, and a draftsman for map making. Two other men of science, lieutenants from Spanish ships, joined them at Cartagena on the Caribbean coast. It was an undertaking planned according to the best standards of the time.

It is interesting to notice that this study was carried on in spite of the fact that France was at war; or, as Condamine puts it in more elegant phrase, "whilst his Majesty's [Louis XV's] armies flew from one end of Europe to the other for the assistance of his allies, his mathematicians, dispersed over the surface of the earth, were at work under the Torrid and Frigid zones for the improvement of the sciences and the common benefit of all nations."

The scientists did their work against almost incredible odds. The observations required constant measuring of mountain heights, experiments at different levels with thermometers and barometers, fixing signals on summits and then checking them from other heights, and recording the swing of a pendulum at different altitudes. Quito is in a valley surrounded by snow-

covered volcanoes, some of which were then in erup-
tion at the time. Condamine climbed Mount Pichincha,
nearly 16,000 feet high, made a journey up the "River
of Emeralds," and went on an exploring trip as far south
as Lima. They were trying to measure a degree on the
earth's surface, and to do so they must check with the
stars constantly, making their observations in a sky
"very unfavorable to astronomers," as Condamine remarks. He had been working six months in a desert far
south of Quito, "struggling both night and day," when
the triumphant end came. In March, 1743, he received
word from one of his fellow scientists, far to the north,
that on a given series of nights he had been able to make
observations on the position of a certain star. On those
same nights Condamine had been able to make similar
observations for the same star. The record was thus
completed from both north and south, and the distance
could be taken. They had charted a distance on the
meridian three degrees in length, which meant that,
roughly estimated, they had surveyed a distance of two
hundred miles, high among the mountain peaks of the
Andes. It was a tremendous contribution to the sum of
knowledge.

If Condamine had gone straight home by the quickest
route, the story would have ended there and been buried
for all time in the dry, mathematical records of science.

But Condamine was not that kind of person. The men had not gotten on well together. They had put their work through, not letting their dislike of one another interfere. Now they wanted to separate, and the broad continent of South America gave them every chance.

Condamine decided to come back across that continent, traveling along the Amazon River; and, being the man he was, he chose to come by the least known and most difficult of the three possible routes. He intended to map the river, and it would be much more worth while to go where other men had not gone. So to his just completed service to science he added a survey of the great river and its tributaries which puts him at the forefront of South American explorers. Father Fritz had done his best with such knowledge as he had and with his missionary calling as his main task. Condamine was the first thoroughly trained scientist to go into the interior. Moreover, he kept full records and published them after his return to Paris in 1745. This account made the regions known in Europe and thus sent other explorers into the districts of which he had told his tales.

One of those tales was of crossing rivers on the terrifying Inca bridges. Back in the days of one of the first Inca kings, long before the white men appeared, the first of these bridges woven of reeds or willows had been constructed, and the pattern had been copied all along the western coast. The conquering Spaniards could hardly have won their way so quickly without these bridges, which they found waiting for their use. The first ones had been swung across narrow mountain defiles, fastened to rocks on either side. Those in the Upper Amazon basin hung by large cables from trees on the riverbanks. Those which Condamine had to cross were one hundred and fifty feet long, an open network with the bottom strewn with reeds, lest a man's foot slip through. When a person started to cross, adding his weight to that of the structure, it would begin to swing back and forth, high above the waters. A white man, tempted to draw back and proceed slowly and fearfully on the swaying ropes, would look down to find the natives laughing at his timidity. They passed over them running, laden with all the baggage taken from the backs of the mules, which were pushed into the waters and forced to swim across.

Dangers multiplied as he went on. He had his Indians make a reed raft for himself and his instruments, and as he rode it he was caught in a whirlpool in which he swung round and round for an hour and some minutes. He would never have come out alive if four of his Indians had not climbed on a rock and thrown him ropes, then towed the raft out.

He was interested in everything he saw and tested everything that came his way. So when he saw the Indians drawing a "most singular resin" from a tree, heating it, and then smearing it on their foot coverings, he asked them why they did it. To keep out dampness, they told him. He tested the coverings and found that water did run off them. They showed him the trees from which the milky fluid could be drawn, and he made his own experiments with the sticky stuff, until at last he, too, had waterproofed his shoes and a coat.

The usual story of rubber is familiar to everyone: how Columbus saw the liquid coming from a tree in the West Indies; how early explorers told of natives of Mexico and Central America playing ball with lumps of the hardened stuff; how an English scientist, Priestley, noted in 1770 that a piece of this substance from South America rubbed off pencil marks on paper and so named it "rubber," and how waterproof garments were called "mackintoshes" because Charles Mackintosh, in the early 1820s, managed to spread the stuff between two layers of cloth. But one picture is left out, that of Charles Condamine, fussing over his smoky fire in the Amazon jungle, with his Indians helping and teaching him, until his shoes and his cloth were waterproofed, and bringing those samples back to France when he came home from his journeyings. It was through him that rubber became widely known, though only as a curious, interesting tree product.

He brought home quinine plants, too, packed in earth in a box and carried on the shoulders of one of his Indians all the long journey to the coast. Those were to be grown in the king's garden in Paris. He got poisoned arrows from the Indians and exhibited them to his hosts when he finally came out to civilization on the Atlantic coast. A single prick on the wing of a domestic fowl brought death within a few minutes, although the weapons were more than a year old. Powerful poison that was, compounded by the Indians according to the rules and magic of their ancestors.

Condamine saw and studied smallpox in South America and took an active part in the argument for inoculation against the disease which came up in his later years. At Quito he had taken time, during the seven years of labor on his main project, to make a careful study of Inca ruins. After his return to France he published descriptions of these buildings, with theories as to how they were constructed.

What did such a man contribute toward the opening up of South America? More than if he had been a Spaniard, perhaps, for he made the regions which he had visited known in a wide circle. Spain tended to keep her colonies and their products to herself. Science has no national boundaries. Condamine's report roused great interest in practically unknown territory. It opened the door for others to follow him, and every expedition did its part in bringing the South American countries into the family of nations.

Don Ambrosio O'Higgins

THE IRISHMAN WHO BECAME A VICEROY

IT READS LIKE A BOY'S SUCCESS STORY, this tale of a poor Irish lad who came to South America in 1770 and won by his own ability the highest office in the country, an office gained by appointment by King Charles III of Spain. But there is much more here than a quick rise to fortune. Ambrose O'Higgins, whom the Spanish-speaking people called "Don Ambrosio," did much for his adopted country during the

95

last years of Spanish rule, besides contributing a son, Bernardo, who led in the struggle for independence.

In Ireland Ambrose was a village lad, a serving boy running errands for the lady of Dangan Castle in County Meath, which is in the southeastern part of the country. He went into the army while he was still very young but failed to get the promotion he expected, and so was ready to go to Spain when an uncle, in the church there, offered to help him toward an education and to a priesthood if he desired. When the time for that choice came he had made up his mind to go out to the New World, of which many reports came to Spain through travelers and traders. Arriving at Buenos Aires, Argentina, he went immediately across the continent to the west coast, where the wealthier cities were.

A New World has many chances for an ambitious youth. Perhaps back in the old country Ambrose O'Higgins had known Irish peddlers who went from village to village with their packs of goods on their backs, getting a welcome wherever they stopped. He had picked up a knowledge of Spanish during his time of study and now began as a traveling peddler, carrying a little stock of goods between Chile and Peru on the west coast. There were no easy routes along the coast. When he left the cities and towns behind he had to go on narrow mountain paths or across barren deserts. But he was a sturdy young man who persevered in whatever he undertook, and he had a gift for trade. Soon he set up a little shop in Lima, Peru, capital for the great viceroyalty of Peru, which extended northward to Quito and southward to Chile.

O'Higgins seems to have won notice from the Spanish officials who governed the country by selling supplies to their army. He had come to Peru at a fortunate time. King Charles III of Spain was a wise ruler who did much for the Spanish-American colonies. There had been a bad practice of discouraging trade except with the mother country. This was to be one of the chief causes of the Wars of Independence. But King Charles permitted trade between the different parts of the empire and particularly between Peru and Chile on the west and Buenos Aires on the east. New cross-continent trade routes were being established. But the route across the Andes from Chile was a dangerous one at all seasons and particularly so in the winter season. One of O'Higgins' first public services was the help he gave to army men in the building of cabins of stone or brick at intervals along the mountain paths, where men and their mules could take refuge during storms.

Soon he was in the army, first in the engineering corps and then as a military officer. Here he had a

chance for active service in fighting against the Araucanians, the unsubdued and troublemaking Indians of
southern Chile who had never yielded to the white
men or made with them a lasting peace. Word of the
young captain's abilities, and of his knowledge of the
country and its people, went across the seas to the king,
who appointed him in 1788 to the high office of captain-
general of Chile, a position which none but a Spaniard
had ever held. This man of Irish birth was really more
of a South American than most of the Spanish officials
who administered the empire, for he had married a
Chilean lady and spoke his new language as fluently as
his native tongue. Moreover, his interest was in developing the country, not in receiving honor for himself and
then going back wealthier than he had come to the
homeland of Spain, as was the case with many of the
governing Spaniards.

In Chilean histories O'Higgins is given the title of
the "Great Captain-general." Most of the governors
stayed fairly close to the cities and the few traveled
routes, devoting themselves chiefly to the southern part
of the country, where the border must be kept well
defended because of the Indians. O'Higgins went into
the north, not hesitating to take time to study the needs
of the common people and seek means to better their
condition.

His efforts and attempted reforms were not very successful. He seems to have had a faith which matches that of modern times in agricultural experiments to be carried out by the government, and the conservative Chilean landowners did not like either change or government supervision. He found small sugar plantations in the northern valleys and sought to create larger ones. But the experiment failed after three or four years. He also tried to extend the growing of rice and to introduce the cultivation of tobacco. In the latter case he ran up against a royal monopoly. The crown and the crown alone had control of all tobacco growing. The thing to notice is, however, not that he sometimes failed, but that he tried. It was not the custom for Spanish captain-generals of those days to be making efforts to improve the lot of the people.

Another of his reforms was even more courageous and in the modern spirit. The Indians who worked in the mines and on the great plantations were little better than slaves. In the early days of Spanish occupation a system had been set up by which owners of great estates were given control of the Indians living on their land. This was necessary at the time, if the Indians were to be forced to work. Now, after a couple of years, there was no need for such forced labor. O'Higgins would have been glad to abolish the whole system. He did insist on its reform, so that the natives would have their rights better protected.

As he journeyed up and down the long, narrow strip of country which is Chile, the thing that impressed him most was the need of roads. Practically all travel outside the few towns and cities was on horseback or muleback. During his first three years in office the governor went back and forth several times over the ninety-mile path between his capital city of Santiago and its port of Valparaiso and made up his mind that if the country was to become more prosperous, there must be a road wide enough for horse-drawn carts and carriages between these two important centers.

But what a fight he had ahead of him to get such a road built! Such projects had no place under the comfortable, easygoing Spanish rule of the colonies, and none but an energetic Irishman would have put this one through. The governing assembly objected to the expense. The owners of land objected to having a public road pass through their estates. Both of these were objections which were to be expected, but the third came near halting even O'Higgins. No one was willing to perform the heavy, backbreaking labor required for the building of the road. The governor had the greatest trouble in getting workmen and in keeping them after he had hired them. The number of men he could get was so small that he finally had to begin on a few of the most needed sections, with the hope that when they were completed, labor could be found to finish the task.

It is so easy for us of modern times to take it for granted that, in the course of the opening up of a country, roads are built. If it were not for a distinguished visitor who came to Chile at this time, we should know little of the odds against which this Irish governor of a Spanish province struggled. But George Vancouver, on his way home from his famous voyage to the Sandwich Islands and to Alaska in search of a Northwest Passage, sailed into the harbor of Valparaiso at this time and traveled over the road while it was still in the process of building.

Vancouver's account of his visit to O'Higgins is one of the most interesting reports of the cities of the west coast in those days. The sea captain was thirty-seven years old in this year of 1794. He had spent his life, since he was fifteen, in exploration, beginning with an Antarctic voyage with Captain Cook. He had now been away from England on "South Sea" voyaging for four years. At the California ports where he had touched, on his way south from Puget Sound, he had had his first news of the French Revolution, then in progress. His coming into Valparaiso harbor was a forced landing, made only because his battered vessel was in need of emergency repairs. He sailed in with considerable misgivings, since it was well understood that the Spaniards did not encourage the visits of foreign vessels to their west-coast ports. Spain wanted to guard its profitable trade, and in these days the king and his counselors were afraid to have their colonials get any news of the spread of republican ideas which were sweeping through Europe.

Captain Vancouver tells in his journal of his approach to the Chilean coast. The prospect was forbidding, with rude cliffs and precipices along the shore, no tree to be seen, and the snowy summits of the Andes in the background. Then the vessel rounded a point, and here was the bay, with several merchant ships anchored. Rising from the water, on steep slopes, was the town of Valparaiso, "neat and of considerable extent," with churches and forts.

"We were again approaching the civilized world," Vancouver wrote.

The misgivings of the visitors were soon at an end. Vancouver sent an officer ashore, who returned with the good news that the present governor of the town was Señor Alava, brother of a friend of Captain Vancouver's at Monterrey, a little settlement on the California coast, where they had recently touched. As soon as the officer returned to the boat with this information

Captain Vancouver had a salute of thirteen guns fired, and a like salute of welcome was returned by the fort on shore. Visits of courtesy were exchanged, and Señor Alava sent a message off at once to Governor O'Higgins, announcing the arrival of the Englishmen. That gentleman sent back promptly a letter of congratulations on the success of Vancouver's present voyage and an escort of two dragoons, who were to bring the captain and his party to "St. Jago," as Santiago was then called. O'Higgins' thoughtfulness was shown in his choice of these men, for they were natives of Ireland, though long in New Spain, and so well able to make the Englishmen feel at home.

Captain Vancouver hesitated, but the invitation was urgent, and the repairs to the damaged mainmast would take several days. When he decided to make the journey he was surprised at the elaborate preparations made to go ninety miles. There would be no suitable accommodations along the way, so their hosts had to provide bedding, seats, tables, utensils for cooking, and a tent. These were packed on the backs of twelve mules, and the cavalcade started.

The old road was a mere beaten track, but the new one was to be wide. It had been begun in 1792, but now, two years later, only a few sections were completed. As they rode along they could watch the men at work widening the narrow mule path, which led up and down through the mountains. There were no wheelbarrows for carting away the earth which they were digging out. Instead two men would spread the hide of an ox on the ground and shovel on it as much earth as they thought they could move. Then they would draw the corners together and pull the hide to the road's edge, to be distributed for the making of a border or tipped over the brink into the valley below. The rocky parts were being blasted away by gunpowder, but the pieces of rock were being tossed away instead of being broken up by hand power and used for roadbed.

South America has always been a land of contrasts, and never more so than in the days of the Spanish empire, when the natives lived as they always had and the ruling Spaniards repeated as nearly as they could the manner of life of their distant homeland. There were contrasts, too, that belonged to the country. Vancouver tells of stopping overnight in hovels where they slept on blankets spread on the bare earth floor, and cooking the poultry, eggs, potatoes, onions, and other vegetables in utensils of silver. This was a country of mines, and silver was the metal most easily obtained. The fresh vegetables and fruits were delicious and particularly welcome to the voyagers after their long stay aboard ship. As they came nearer to the city they left behind the brown mountainsides and began to see plantations and vineyards.

Captain Vancouver had questioned about accepting the governor's invitation because of the shabby clothes of himself and his fellow officers. At the end of a four-year voyage no one of them had any uniforms fit for ordinary use, much less for such an occasion as visiting a Spanish governor in his palace. For the trip they had dressed in their roughest clothes, knowing that such uniforms as they had were too rotten to stand horseback riding. Outside the city they were met by two officers with fresh horses, with fine saddles and bridles, the saddlecloths fringed with gold and silver lace. The Englishmen were embarrassed to mount these animals and proceed in their misfit coats and hats through the streets of the city, where the people had assembled to see them pass.

But when they came to the palace the gracious Irish-Spanish governor was able to put them at their ease. He was so glad to see them and so grateful to them for coming that they were repaid for the discomforts of the journey. At an elaborate supper of hot dishes he pressed them with compliments on their remarkable voyage and questions about the new lands they had discovered in the northwest. The same experience was repeated the next morning, which happened to be Sunday, the day on which the governor always had a reception in his fine audience chamber. Again they were embarrassed by their shabby appearance among the elegantly dressed guests, but Governor O'Higgins lost no opportunity to tell about their remarkable discoveries and dwell on their bravery and skill as seamen. Once more they noticed one of the strange contrasts which they had found on every hand in this land. The dinner at the palace was served on a table built of common boards, not too well put together, but all the serving dishes were of solid silver.

The visit over, Captain Vancouver returned to his boat and sailed on around the Horn and back to England. But in his reports of his voyage, both spoken and written, he gave a vivid description of his visit to Chile, with warm tributes to Governor O'Higgins. It was by such exchanges of courtesy that Englishmen came to know of South America and feel friendly to its people, even though there was resentment at the way in which Spain was trying to hold the continent from all comers, as if it were her own private property.

O'Higgins was soon called to higher honors. In 1796 he was promoted to be viceroy of Peru, the most important governing office on the continent. As if to make up for his lowly, foreign birth, the Spanish court showered him with titles. He was made Marquis of Orono and Count of Balenar, as well as brigadier-general and then major-general. But the people still called him "Don Ambrosio," and he remained the same simple, friendly, capable administrator.

He contributed so much service to his adopted land that one must pick and choose in the reporting, or else the list becomes too long. There was the building of roads, with the construction of a great wall to hold back the river which threatened in floodtimes to overflow the city of Santiago. There was his effort to better the lot of the poorer folk of the mountain districts, for whom no one had had any particular concern before. He did a remarkable job in bringing the fine, independent Araucanians into harmonious relations with the government of Chile. It was no light matter to end a two-hundred-year feud which had brought constant bloodshed on both sides. By all these means he left Chile in far better condition than he found it, and so won his place as if he had been a Chilean by birth instead of by his own choice.

If there had been more viceroys like him, the Wars of Independence, in which his son took an active part, might have been less bitter.

Bolívar and His Marches

"IF NATURE OPPOSES US, WE WILL BATTLE
WITH HER, AND COMPEL HER TO
OBEY US!"—*Simón Bolívar*

ONE NAME STANDS ABOVE ALL OTHER
names in South America, the name of Simón Bolívar,
the Liberator. His statue is in hundreds of public
squares; his portrait is on the walls of public buildings
from one end of the continent to the other. Coins bear
his name. His words are quoted in legislative assemblies,
as Washington's and Lincoln's are quoted by us to this
day. Five republics count him the author of their independence, one of them bearing his name.

If Bolívar had known how the peoples of widely separated republics would unite in remembering him, he would have been comforted, for it was his dream to bring these peoples together. He saw South America as a whole and so was able to take a leading part in freeing it from Spanish rule. If he had seen it only in its separate parts, as did many of the leaders of different regions, he could never have done what he did. The sign of his seeing it as a whole, and planning his campaigns with that vision, is the series of marches which he undertook with his armies. For him the terrific barriers of mountain, jungle, desert, and river, which Nature had placed in his way, were only obstacles to be overcome as he passed on his unswerving course. For him differences of race did not matter. He gave the Indians in his armies the same treatment that he gave the whites, and they followed him with a loyalty that ended only with death. He gave to those who worked with him a new view of the continent in which they lived and of the peoples who made it up.

I

Simón Bolívar was a Venezuelan, born in Caracas July 24, 1783, of a wealthy colonial family. But while he was still a boy he came up against a barrier which

he could not overcome. Although his family had wealth
and position in Venezuela, although pure Spanish blood
ran in his veins, with a rich inheritance of family honors
in Spain, he had been born in the colony. That gave him
a social standing below that of any Spanish official who
came out from the mother country to govern Venezuela.

There were restraints that every Creole, as a person
of Spanish blood but South American birth was called,
ran up against before they were grown to manhood.
Spaniards could travel from one part of the South
American empire to another, if they so desired. But
for a Creole to make such trips was well-nigh impossible. Neither he nor any member of his family could
start up and go to New Granada (now Colombia) by
way of the Caribbean, nor around through Panama to
the west-coast cities, nor south to Buenos Aires on the
Plata River, without a passport. And the Spanish
officials were instructed by the king and his counselors
to withhold such papers except when some urgent need
arose.

Young Bolívar could go to Europe, to Spain, which
was the home of his ancestors. He did this, as soon as he
was old enough, for such was the custom for lads of
aristocratic families who desired an education. There,
after a period of years, he made his resolve to give his

life to the freeing of his native land from the chains which bound her. With other young colonials, he felt that the time had come for her to follow the example of her northern neighbors, who had freed themselves by the American Revolution some thirty years earlier.

He came back to Caracas full of enthusiasm for revolution and worked with other patriots toward that Declaration of Independence of July 5, 1811, by which the First Republic of Venezuela was set up. For thirteen months he fought under General Miranda to maintain that republic. It was at that time, after the terrible earthquake of 1812 in Caracas, that he made his famous remark, "If Nature opposes us, we will battle with her and compel her to obey us!" That was to be his cry for all the rest of his life.

The First Republic failed. The patriots were defeated by Spanish armies, and young Bolívar was sent into exile, while his general was held in prison. So little was the young officer regarded by the Spanish leaders of the opposing army that there was no objection to his departure. The royalist commander, General Monteverde, was willing to have him go free, saying contemptuously, "Give the fool his passport and let him go."

Bolívar did not go far. From a little Dutch-owned island north of Venezuela he looked back toward South

America and began to think beyond his own province. The revolt in Venezuela had been put down for the time. But there were other provinces which were beginning to rebel. The march of Napoleon's armies into Spain had given the signal. To be ruled by a French Bonaparte, the conqueror's brother Joseph, was not to be borne by the colonists. Bolívar saw that it was not simply Venezuelan freedom for which he must work.

Within a few weeks he was back on South American soil, but not in Venezuela. He had crossed by sailing ship to Cartagena, which was the northern port of New Granada, to try to persuade the patriots of that province to go over and help the Venezuelans. By a public letter of appeal, added to his own passionate arguments, he made the people of Cartagena look beyond their own borders. He warned them that they should act for their own defense by sending an army across the mountains instead of waiting for the Spanish general to gather his forces and come over to attack them. It was the old-new cry to take the military offensive instead of staying comfortably on the defensive.

The black-haired young patriot-captain won the people to his way of thinking. Three months from the time of his landing, Bolívar was on his way up the

Magdalena River with a small force of men who were ready to follow him across the mountains to Venezuela.

This first of Bolívar's famous marches was a triumph of human endurance. The soldiers worked their way up the river through a green wilderness. Then they came up from the hot jungle into cold, wind-swept heights. The mountains to be crossed were ten, twelve, fifteen thousand feet high. For ten long days and nights Bolívar and his men pressed on, wandering without shelter and with little food along the blind trails through the passes. The painful *soroche*, the mountain sickness, attacked them. The cold chilled them to the bone. But always the young commander was helping, encouraging, inspiring the weary men. Haggard, worn, with his black eyes burning like lights in his face, he was at the front of the line, in the middle, at the rear, wherever the need of him was greatest.

The little army came over the crest of those northern Andes and would have halted for a few days to get themselves back to their normal health and strength. But they could not stop. Royalist troops were waiting in mountain stations on the other side. The patriots had to begin to fight at once, before they recovered their strength. Yet they won those skirmishes and moved on to other battles, as they marched on through western Venezuela.

Ninety days after he left New Granada Bolívar arrived in triumph at the gates of Caracas. The Spanish forces were defeated. He was ready to help the Venezuelans to set up the Second Republic. At the city gates he exchanged his ragged uniform for one more suitable for a parade and stepped into a flower-decked carriage which was waiting for him. Twelve beautiful daughters of citizens were waiting to draw that carriage slowly through the streets, while the people crowded the sidewalks and shouted from windows and housetops their welcome to "the Liberator." That was the first time he was greeted by that title, which was to become almost as much a part of him as his name. The honors were shared by the ragged, exhausted soldiers from New Granada. The men of the west had come across the mountains to help the patriots of the east. These two parts of the continent had been brought together as never before.

II

That triumph was brief. The patriot armies were soon fighting again, this time against all the forces that the aroused Spanish generals could throw against them. A new leader, Tomás Boves, came up with an army from the southern llanos, those grassy plains along the

Orinoco River. He and his men were a wild group, ravaging the country. There was no safety for man, woman, or child as their cruel hordes swept on.

For six months the patriots held out, disputing every mile of the advance. In the end they had to yield. The city of Caracas was abandoned, and Bolívar led another march across the mountains, this time over an eastern range which lay between the city and the distant shores of the Atlantic. This was a flight of men, women, and children, civilians as well as soldiers, refugees fleeing before the enemy. Venezuelan artists have pictured Bolívar in the midst of that disastrous march, riding with his head bowed, his long cloak covering his body, as he brought the remnant of the survivors along the hard and dangerous paths.

Again Bolívar must go into exile, this time with his own people turned against him. Many of the patriot leaders, who had been jealous of his popularity, blamed him for the defeat. He went back by sailboat to New Granada, where he was warmly welcomed even though he was defeated. But for his spirit the healing of that welcome was brief. The royalists, reinforced from Spain, gathered their armies and inflicted disastrous defeats on the patriots of that province. They were determined to wipe out all traces of revolution in the entire northern portion of the continent.

Once more Bolívar must leave South America, now with a price put on his head by the Spaniards. He took refuge in the British island of Jamaica and lived there in poverty, fed and sheltered through the charity of friends, and with his health shattered. This was his period of deepest discouragement. Those who looked on feared that he had come to the end of his strength and courage.

But courage came back to him, and with it a wider vision. Now he saw that his work must be expanded if it was to succeed. Not Venezuela only, nor New Granada, but all Spanish South America must be freed from overseas rule. He was ready now to write a "letter to all the world," setting forth his dream of a new, free America.

"I wish above all else," he wrote, "to see the formation in America of the greatest nation of the world— the greatest not so much because of its size as because of its glory and liberty!"

He had gone beyond the thought of the single continent of South America and was talking of a Pan-American future. He was dreaming of a congress at Panama, where all the republics of America, both North and South, would meet for conference, with representatives of the other parts of the world coming for conference. He was talking of a "united America,

Mother of Republics." Yet at that moment Spain had put down most of the movements toward independence in the colonies and was considering the revolutions suppressed. They were reckoning without the exile in Jamaica.

III

General Bolívar returned to stage his attack from a new place. No longer was he starting at the northern ports. He was making a new headquarters on the Orinoco River, at Angostura (soon to be named Ciudad Bolívar, Bolívar City), and calling a congress there to set up once more the Venezuelan republic.

At this place, two hundred and fifty miles inland from the Atlantic but still accessible by water for supplies from other countries, he gathered his forces and planned new campaigns. The congress met and formed a constitution. At a dinner of legislators and public officials he made his most dramatic speech.

He had been telling his plans, and others had been listening. Excited by the talk and intoxicated by the thrill of his own dreams, the Liberator leaped from his seat at the head of the board to stand on the table top. Between the lines of his astonished guests he walked its length, with dishes breaking beneath his feet.

"Even so," he shouted, "I shall march from the

Atlantic to the Pacific, from Panama to Cape Horn, until the last Spaniard is expelled!"

That was oratory; but it was turned into cold, sober, military planning a few months later. In that interval Bolívar had met and won to his side General Páez, leader of the fighters from the llanos, a picturesque individual who had risen from being a cowboy to the command of a motley horde of devoted soldiers. The two had joined forces and done some fighting together. But Bolívar's armies had suffered a succession of crushing defeats in northern Venezuela. The Spanish generals did not see how he was able even to keep on, much less win even passing victories. Bolívar knew better than they his weaknesses. In the whole of that country the combined forces of his men and those of Páez numbered hardly more than seven thousand, while the Spanish commander had seventeen thousand well-trained veterans. The odds were heavily against the patriot leader, so heavily that his defeat seemed a matter of months if not of weeks.

Bolívar called his leaders to a conference at a little hut in a village on the inland plains. English officers and Irish were there, as well as the colonial leaders, for a great number of foreign soldiers, legionnaires fresh from the Napoleonic Wars, had come across the ocean to fight with the South Americans. There was no

furniture in the hut except the skulls of cattle, dried
and bleached in the sun, which could serve for seats
for those who did not stand or sit on the floor. Bolívar
walked back and forth, gesticulating nervously with
his long, slender hands. He looked much older than
he was, for deep wrinkles had come in his forehead at
an early age. But he was active and alert. These men
who had fought with him knew his great reserves of
strength, which kept him from showing any sign of
fatigue, even after exacting marches and hard campaigns.

Talking fast, to get his ideas across to them as
rapidly as possible, he outlined a new plan. Over in
the province of New Granada the royalist troops
were not so numerous and were more scattered because
of the size of the country. There were patriot troops,
too, under good leaders. Why should they not go over
there, leaving a small company to harass and deceive
the Spaniards into thinking the entire army still in the
region?

The answer could be read in the faces of the men.
New Granada was a third of the way farther across
the continent, and between it and them stretched hundreds of miles of llanos, now turned almost into swamps
by the rainy season, with the mountain slopes of the
high Andes at their end. Nature had given the answer
to that question as to why the two countries should

not join hands. But to Bolívar this was a familiar problem, to which he had given his answer long ago, at the time of the Caracas earthquake. If Nature opposed him, he would compel her.

Hours passed while the men argued. Through all the discussion Bolívar held to his point. "We must cross the Andes if we are to gain the victory," he declared. In the end he won them over. It was a gay, impulsive Irishman by the name of Rooke, one of his best lieutenants, who swung them to the final yielding.

"Lead the way," he cried. "Say the word, General Bolívar, and I'll march with you not only over the Andes but right down to Patagonia—even to Cape Horn!"

The tale of that march is history, written in the hearts and minds of the South American people. For weeks the men made their way across the llanos, struggling through the wet lands, trying to ford the swollen rivers, with lives lost all along the route by one tragedy and another.

Then they came to the mountain slopes, and again, as he had on that first march of his, the Liberator was leading men from the plains, men of the tropics, up into the bitter heights of the Andes. The march would have been hard enough if they could have made the crossing of those lofty regions unopposed, but as they neared their goal one of their scouts brought word that the pass through which they had expected to go was held by a small Spanish force, on guard to keep any enemy troops from marching through.

With that crossing blocked, there was only one other way. That night they must do the impossible. They must go over the Paramo, a lofty, wind-swept region of eternal snow, where only occasional mountain climbers ever ventured. All their previous hardships were in vain if they could not get over into New Granada, and this was the only way.

Many died during that wild night, falling from precipices as they tried to cling to the narrow paths, dropping by the way and freezing, perishing from mountain sickness. But the remnant of the army came over and staggered down the other side of the mountain to the villages below. There they were met as if they were ghosts, not living men. Surely they could not have crossed by that route, which was not a route but an impassable barrier.

Within a few days these men revived to fight. Patriots of New Granada, rallied by one of Bolívar's officers whom he had sent ahead weeks earlier, joined them in the Battle of Boyacá, one of the chief and decisive battles of the Wars of Independence. Bolívar and his victorious troops were soon entering the capital, Bogotá, from which the Spanish governor fled in haste at their approach.

Once more Bolívar had proved that the mountain walls which separated the countries of South America could be crossed, not only by single travelers or small groups of traders, but by large numbers of men. The Andes were no longer an insurmountable barrier.

IV

From Bogotá Bolívar looked south to Quito, where one of the first revolts against Spanish rule had been made a few years back. He could not go to join and help those brave patriots, for he must lead an army back to Venezuela. He had split the northern part of the Spanish empire into two parts, but he must go back and follow up his victories. In 1821 he won, on the plains of Carabobo, his second great victory. The power of Spain in the north was broken. But still there was Quito, with Peru to the south.

Bolívar had already sent to Quito one of his best generals, Antonio Sucre, who was fighting to drive the Spanish garrisons out and deliver the region. As soon as the Liberator could leave the government of the northern provinces in other hands, he went south with a small army over a long and difficult route to join his general. In May of 1822 Sucre won the Battle of Pichincha and was able to enter Quito as victor. Within a month Bolívar joined him.

Meanwhile General San Martín of Argentina had come up to deliver Peru from Spanish control. Bolívar went there to complete the work, while Sucre led armies up into the mountains and won the Battle of Ayacucho, the great and final victory which ended, in 1824, the Wars of Independence. The new republic established in Upper Peru was named Bolivia in honor of the Liberator, who had led five countries to freedom.

Bolívar's dream of a united group of nations did not come to pass. To him it seemed in the next few years as if he had failed. "I have plowed in the sea," he declared mournfully, as he suffered from the dissension within and between the new republics.

History tells another story. The mountain paths which had been traveled by armies could be used in times of peace. Spain had tried to keep the different districts apart. Bolívar had brought them together. Others were to carry on the work. But before we come to the after-revolution days we turn to the story of what was going on in the south during the years of the northern campaigns. There another great leader, General San Martín, the Saint of the Sword, as they called him, had his dream of a South America united to throw off Spanish rule. By coming up from the south to Peru, he made the final triumph possible.

San Martín
Crosses the Andes

"WHAT SPOILS MY SLEEP IS NOT THE
STRENGTH OF THE ENEMY, BUT HOW TO
PASS THOSE IMMENSE MOUNTAINS."

San Martín

IF MOUNTAINS HAVE SOULS, AS THE IN-
dians declare they do, the high peaks of the Andes
chain, which divides South America from north to
south, must have looked down, in the early nineteenth
century, with surprise and some displeasure at the little,
puny human beings who were tracking through their
passes. For long centuries their snowy walls had kept
the peoples of the different lands in their native places,

with only a few bold individuals going back and forth, singly or in small groups, over the narrow paths. But now whole processions of men came winding up the slopes, with mules carrying on their backs strange loads, and went down on the opposite sides of the ranges. The power of the mountains was beginning to go if these human beings could run back and forth as if they were not there.

The mountains could not know the suffering that these journeys cost. They could not know that only the passion for freedom would drive men out of their comfortable valleys to defy their heights. Only for such a cause would Bolívar and his armies have crossed and recrossed the Andes of the north. Only for such a cause did General San Martín make his famous crossing from Argentina to Chile, a mountain march that ranks in military annals with Hannibal's and Napoleon's famous marches across the Alps.

José de San Martín had his military training in Europe. Born in a little village on Argentina's northeastern frontier in 1778, two years after the North American Declaration of Independence, he went with his father, a captain in the Spanish army, to Madrid when he was a small boy seven years old. When he was only eleven he enlisted as a cadet, beginning twenty years of service in Spain's armies. During the latter part of that time it was most active service, for he was fighting against Napoleon's troops. He learned all that Europe could teach him about military service, and he had a mind which could absorb what he learned.

When news of the beginning of Argentine revolt against Spain came to him in Europe, he made plans at once to return. Arriving in Buenos Aires in 1812, he organized a patriot regiment and helped for a time in campaigns near the coast. Then, because he was the best-trained officer in the army, he was sent inland to Upper Peru (now Bolivia) in the center of the continent. The center of the Spanish power was Lima, Peru, over the mountains toward the coast. The only well-traveled trade route across the continent came from Lima through Upper Peru and then dropped down across the country to Buenos Aires on the Atlantic coast. By that route the viceroy in Lima was beginning to send royalist armies, who were to come over to the region around Buenos Aires and bring the rebels back under Spanish rule. But the rebels, meanwhile, had sent an army up into this high country to hold the Spaniards back. General San Martín went up to command that army.

As he served with that Army of the North this wise general came to the decision that he was in the wrong place. Victory would not come by the present plan of defensive action. Here the Spaniards were at their strongest. They might be held back by this Argentinean army, but there could be no successful advance. Peru could not be conquered by this back-door route, and while the Spanish government held Peru there could be no final victory for any South American nation.

Up in that mountain region, while he went quietly and efficiently about his duties, General San Martín conceived his daring plan. He called it his "secret" in a letter to a friend, for he did not advertise it. He did not want the Spaniards to get wind of so bold a plan, and he knew too well that it would find many critics back in Buenos Aires. San Martín merely got himself transferred to Mendoza, a town much farther to the south, on the eastern edge of the Andes, as they lay over against Chile. There he went quietly to work to carry out his idea.

San Martín's method was as different from that of the eager, impetuous Bolívar as black is from white. The Venezuelan depended on bold dashes, made after quick decisions. San Martín moved slowly and cautiously. He was a man of long military training and experience, and his theory was that success came through long and thorough preparation. Without letting his final project be known, he began to train an army and create war materials. Not till the people were discouraged by years of defeats in the northern regions did he reveal his purpose of taking that army over the Andes to Chile and then north to the front door of Peru. It was a plan of carrying the offensive into the heart of the enemy's territory instead of waiting for the enemy to strike.

By the time the general did make known his plan he had gained able recruits from the seacoast province of Chile. These patriot leaders and soldiers had attempted a revolution and been defeated by troops sent down from Peru. Among those who had been forced to flee was Bernardo O'Higgins, son of the late viceroy. To these Chileans the idea of taking an army over the Andes, for the rescue of their native land, did not seem unreasonable. But to many of San Martín's superiors in Buenos Aires such a plan was too wild to be considered. One fought on one's own soil, to free one's own country. To cross the Andes and fight on the Pacific to drive the Spaniards out of Chile was to ask for unnecessary trouble. Let the Chileans fight their own battles, they said. But San Martín kept quietly on with his business of training his army, and there were enough men who agreed with him to give him hope.

In the beginning no one had any faint notion of the preparations which the general considered necessary for such a march. This was to be no haphazard, hasty undertaking. San Martín had too much respect for those gigantic snowy mountains for that. He was going to plan every detail of his assault on those heights.

An army must be fed, and this army would be for many days in barren regions where there were no growing plants or living creatures. The general had a ration prepared, a food made up of beef, dried and pounded to powder, then mixed with fat and Chilean pepper. A soldier could carry in his knapsack enough of these small cakes to feed him for eight days.

There would be ravines to cross where there were no bridges. He had his men copy the Inca bridges of long-past days, some of which were still in use. They took reeds and willows and wove strong cables into portable bridges which could be anchored on each side of a narrow chasm.

An armory was set up, in charge of a mechanical genius whom the general discovered, a friar, Fray Luis Beltrán, who proceeded to train three hundred workmen in his arts. At his forges were produced cartridges, bayonets, horseshoes, gun carriages, and all the other war material required. This was to be no sortie of ill-equipped fighters. Every musket had to be tested, and repaired if it did not work as it should.

Artillery must be taken over the mountains, and Beltrán had special carriages built, at the general's order, for that purpose. The heavy loads of guns were to be slung on the backs of mules in specially reinforced packs.

For months the pleasant valley of Mendoza echoed to the new sounds: the pounding of hammers and the ringing orders of officers to their marching troops. Listening women sewed on uniforms for the men, weaving the cloth first on their looms, and brought their jewels to the general to be turned into money when the supplies threatened to run short.

In his office General San Martín studied the maps made from the sketches which his surveyors brought him. They had gone over every pass in the mountains, along a distance of fifteen hundred miles, and brought back careful accounts and accurate drawings of the routes. When the time for the march came the general could tell to a day, and almost to an hour, how long it would take each section of his army to go over each intended path.

When the day arrived, after three years of preparation, he took his men to the cathedral for a final service, dedicated their flags for them in an inspiring public service, and sent them out with the words ringing in their ears that consecrated them all to the cause of independence. He had been called the Saint of the Sword before that day. From that hour it was his familiar title.

The men were to go in six detachments. For months San Martín had been endeavoring to mislead the Spanish generals on the other side of the mountains as to his probable routes. He had let their guards seize papers from his scouts and had spread among the Indians the idea that he was going to strike first in the south. He knew that a large number of troops had been massed there to stop him. But his real plan was to go over by two mountain passes not far north of Santiago.

A small detachment of Chilean miners, with a couple of hundred volunteers, was to go far north and capture a Spanish outpost which was poorly guarded. A second column of six hundred soldiers was to cross by a pass farther south. Two small companies, one of twenty-five men, the other of less than a hundred, were to cross by other passes. By this means the Spanish troops would be led to think that the main army might be coming in the rear of any one of these advance companies. Along a front of thirteen hundred miles their officers would be kept uncertain and disturbed, not daring to withdraw any of their men.

The general's timetable was a remarkable piece of planning. The leader of each company had a time schedule giving the length of each day's march, with time allowed for constructing bridges and crossing precipices. He knew where food, water, wood for making fires, and forage for the animals would be found. There were allowances for delays, and couriers were to go between the companies. These men were Chilean muleteers and mountain men, who knew every trail. The soldiers were to be kept in good condition on the march by riding part of the time and walking for the rest of the day's journey.

While these smaller companies were making their way through these four widely separated mountain passes, the main portions of the army were to go over two main passes, the Uspallata Pass (where the Christ of the Andes now stands) and the Los Patos Pass. The former was the only route over which artillery and baggage could be carried. The column of eight hundred men, with these supplies, was to be accompanied by miners and road builders, who could repair the paths where they were in need of attention. These men were to cover one hundred and sixty-five miles in ten days. The other party, led by San Martín, with O'Higgins as his assistant, was to make the longer journey of two hundred and seventy-five miles in seventeen days.

On paper such a plan sounds possible. On level land such marches might be expected to go smoothly. But these marches were over mountain passes, some of which were twelve thousand feet high. The marvel is that the whole operation worked out according to the plan.

The hardships are mentioned in brief sentences in the military reports. The animals suffered most. Six thousand mules and two thirds of the horses died before the journeys' ends were reached. They could not stand the terrific cold and the lack of oxygen on those twelve-thousand-foot heights. But they had done much of the work before they dropped from exhaustion and lack of breath. The men carried on their work. They managed, says the account, to bring all the guns across. The soldiers from the pampas suffered most, for they were unused to mountain climbing. But the Chilean and Argentinean mountaineers knew how to relieve their sufferings from the mountain sickness by simple remedies, bleeding them or giving them onions and garlic or dosing them with wine.

The march began in January, which was the summer season in that below-the-equator country. On February 12, 1817, General San Martín's military machine, so perfectly reassembled, came into action against the surprised Spanish forces. The Battle of Chacabuco was won. The barrier of the Andes had been surmounted, to the utter unbelief of the Spanish generals. They could understand that men might have come through, but that they should have brought their artillery and other equipment with them was beyond belief.

San Martín's work was by no means over. Bernardo

O'Higgins was to go about the work of creating a navy; Admiral Cochrane was to come around from the east coast and man it; and in two years a patriot army, under the general's leadership, was to be landed in Peru. Its victories were to be the forerunner of the final conquest, achieved after the meeting with Bolívar, who came down from the north.

When the Wars of Independence were over, in 1824, South America had been opened up as it had never been before. Where armies could go, trade could follow. When trade was being carried on, there was intercourse and travel. Inventions were being made in England and the United States which were making travel and transportation more rapid. Men from other countries could come in now, as they had never been allowed to do under Spanish rule, and join with the patriot leaders in developing their countries.

William Wheelwright of Newburyport

A YANKEE WHOM SOUTH AMERICA HONORS

A VISITOR FROM THE UNITED STATES
who goes to the beautiful seaport city of Valparaiso,
Chile, is likely to have one embarrassing experience. He
will be taken by his guide to a public square where
stands a fine bronze statue of heroic size and will be
told, "Here is your fellow countryman."

He will gaze at the figure of a benevolent, prosperous-
looking gentleman, obviously American, with round

face and high forehead and far-seeing eyes—a figure such as he might expect to see at home in front of a New England town hall or a public library—and he will read the inscription beneath the statue. But in all probability the name will be unfamiliar to him.

To William Wheelwright
Citizen of the United States
From a Thankful People.

Below those lines he will see four words, which are expected to recall to his mind the reason for the presence of this statue in Valparaiso, when the city's other public spots are adorned by the figures of South American liberators and heroes. But unless he knows more of his South American history than do most of us, those words will help him not at all:

Steam Navigation   Railroads
Telegraphs

Just that, and nothing more!

In Chile those words may be enough to tell the story, but not for us. We need to know far more if we are to claim with pride the fellow American to whom this southern republic has given this honor.

I

South Americans begin the story with the shipwreck that landed William Wheelwright on their shores in the year 1823. But we go back to a small boy (born in 1798) who lived in the fine house of his shipowner father, Captain Ebenezer Wheelwright, on High Street in Newburyport, Massachusetts, which was then a busy seaport, sending its sailing vessels out on long trading voyages.

That boy used to sit at the window of his bedroom, forgetting the lessons which he had been sent upstairs to study while he looked out over the harbor to the dim horizon. There he might see a ship which he had visited the day before, at one of the wharves, go sailing out of sight. Someday, he resolved, he would go on one of those ships. It would be just as soon as he was old enough—and perhaps sooner, if he could get his way.

But William's first trip away from home was not on one of those boats. When he was nine years old his father took him to New York. There, on a never-to-be-forgotten August day in 1807, he stood with the crowd that shouted with excitement as Robert Fulton's *Clermont* steamed up the Hudson River at the rate of five miles an hour, driven by an engine inside it instead of by wind-filled sails. Captain Wheelwright declared that it was all foolishness to think that such a mechanical contraption was anything but a freak invention, a kind of toy that might be useful in smooth river waters. Besides, how could a boat carry fuel enough for a sea voyage, even if the engine could keep the paddle wheels turning in rough weather? No! Sails were good enough for him, Captain Ebenezer said. But his small son was thrilled by this sight and would have given anything in the world to be aboard the *Clermont,* seeing how the machinery worked.

"Steam navigation"—those were the first words of the four, were they not? But that was to come long years after the nine-year-old lad saw that steamboat on the Hudson.

In those years William was to become a sea captain himself and learn all the ways of sailing vessels. His father kept him at school until he was sixteen, insisting on two years at Phillips Academy, Andover, after he had finished at Newburyport. But at sixteen he went as a cabin boy on one of the family vessels and when he got home from that trip shipped again as a common sailor on a boat bound for New Orleans. This time he met real adventure, for the ship went aground off a Caribbean island, and its cargo of lime caught fire. The crew escaped in a leaky small boat which filled with water faster than they could bail it out with their hats. Even the older sailors admitted that it was a miracle that anyone got ashore from that trip.

Adventure seemed to follow young Wheelwright, as probably it did most boys who chose in those days to follow the calling of the sea. There is a tale of his catching a fever and being left behind in a West Indies port, where he nearly died. Another tale is of his being nearly murdered in his bunk, aboard a bark which he was taking to Rio de Janeiro, Brazil, when he was only nineteen years old. He had put down a small mutiny among the men, and on the voyage home one of the rebellious sailors got into his cabin at night and tried to take his revenge.

But the adventure which began his South American life came in the year 1823, when the *Rising Empire*, sixty-five days out of Newburyport, with Wheelwright as captain, ran ashore on a sand bank of the wide Plata River bay, off Buenos Aires. The crew escaped in a longboat, while the valuable cargo of lumber and dry-goods was scattered by the waves and the vessel was pounded to pieces. They managed to reach land after a day and night of strenuous rowing and were lucky in finding, after several hours of walking, an Indian village, where they won for themselves a welcome by presenting three muskets, salvaged by good fortune from the ship.

So Wheelwright began his South American life as a penniless youth of twenty-five, arriving in Buenos Aires with no possessions but the shrunken, sea-stained suit of clothes on his back. It was a bitter blow to his pride, for this was his first trip as captain of a ship and his first voyage as far south as Argentina. But the kindly people who took him into their home comforted him by telling him that his misfortune was a not uncommon one. The wide Plata River bay had been the scene of many such disasters, when experienced pilots, thoroughly familiar with the currents and shoals, were at the helm of their vessels. Fifty years later Wheelwright was to wind up his South American career by getting a better harbor for Buenos Aires, but the discouraged young sea captain of the year 1823 had no power to look ahead to any such event.

Two years and more later he was still remembering his discouragement as he wrote home the letter which was the first to reach his anxious family. They had known of the loss of the ship and of his safe landing, but seem to have had no direct word from him. When the letter did arrive it was from a port on the other side of the continent from Buenos Aires, where it had been picked up by a vessel bound for Salem, Massachusetts. No wonder it was to be one of Wheelwright's goals in later years to shorten the time which it took for mail to go from port to port.

It was a stiff, formal letter, after the custom of those days, but through it we can get a little idea of the young man who sent it.

After the loss of the ship, I became weary and worn out with misfortune. Distance and active business, I hoped, would in some measure obliterate painful memories. The course I pursued has had that effect.

Since my arrival in the Pacific I have not been free from trouble; I have been obliged to combat innumerable difficulties. I have now good prospects, but am far from being elated.

Then comes the sad postscript:

More than two years have elapsed and I hear nothing from home. I am in anxious suspense. Who knows what sad changes may have taken place?

Anyone from the United States who took up his residence in South America in those days was practically cut off from his home, so uncertain were the trips of the trading vessels which were the only means of communication.

It was while young Wheelwright was "weary and worn out with misfortune," after the loss of his ship, that the chance came to him which was to shape his future. A gentleman in Buenos Aires asked him if he would like to go as supercargo on one of his ships which was going around Cape Horn and up the west coast of South America to Chile, and he accepted the offer. It would be a new experience for him to go as supercargo, handling the business end of the venture for the owner instead of attending to the sailing of the ship and its navigating. But he was familiar with the ways of North American trading and was good at figuring, as any man must be to rise from the place of cabin boy to that of captain in nine years. It took a good knowledge of mathematics to work out a vessel's course from the sailing charts and the position of the stars. He should not find it difficult to turn that knowledge to the figuring of costs and wages and profits.

So Wheelwright came to the west coast, and he came at a fortunate time. The Wars of Independence, which had been going on for nearly fifteen years, were almost over, and the ports which Spain had kept so jealously closed to foreign trade were being thrown open by the patriot leaders of the new republics. These men felt grateful to the United States, for our government had helped their cause at a critical time, a couple of years earlier, by giving official recognition to their newly separated nations. Henry Clay had been preaching Pan-American unity in Congress, and President Monroe had announced at the end of the year 1823 (the year when Wheelwright landed in Buenos Aires) the doctrine of "Hands Off the Americas."

Wheelwright did not stay in Chile, for there was a civil war going on there, but went immediately north on the two-thousand-mile sea trip to Guayaquil, and it was well he did so, for this was the best harbor and the busiest seaport on the west coast. Here he could see the opportunity for a young, ambitious businessman to make money in trade and help in the opening up of the country.

II

It is not easy to get a picture of Wheelwright's life in the next few years, which led up to his big enterprises; yet that picture is necessary if we are to understand why he could accomplish what he did.

He did not stay a foreigner and outsider, as many of the businessmen from other countries did in these South American ports. He learned Spanish, so that he talked with the people as if he were a native. He made friends with everyone. In this period following the throwing off of the rule of Spain there were sharp political struggles within the South American republics, often with civil war and bloodshed. An indiscreet foreigner might have gotten into all sorts of difficulties, but Wheelwright never took sides and managed to maintain friendly relations with opposing leaders. It is pleasant to think of this American home as not only a center for discussion but also a refuge for those who were in need of protection when they were on the losing side. The government at Washington recognized his ability and made him United States consul, which was a responsible post for so young a man to hold.

Meanwhile the possibilities of the country were growing on him. As he carried on his coastwise trading, up and down the long Pacific coast, he was studying the opportunities. Spain had discouraged such local trade. The king and his counselors had wanted all the profits they could get from the rich colonies. So they had had the precious metals from the mines and the other valuable exports sent straight to their European ports, and they had forced the colonists to purchase everything from their agents, who imported the goods from Spain and made a tremendous profit from selling them. But now South America was independent, and there could be free trading along the Pacific, as well as with the Argentine ports and the outside world.

Wheelwright did not spend all his time at his office in Guayaquil. There are tales of his going on difficult inland exploring trips—of a dislocated shoulder that was set by a skillful Indian far in the interior, and of a holdup by highwaymen, when his life was in danger.

But his chief interest continued to be the sea. Here, as in few other countries of the world, the ocean was the best channel for both travel and trade. The roads between the republics along the coast, Colombia, Peru, and Chile, were still narrow trails, mule paths which wound up into the mountains; and there were wide stretches of almost impassable desert and jungle. The five-hundred-mile and thousand-mile journeys between the chief cities and ports were best made by water.

Yet sea travel was slow and difficult. The Pacific Ocean had earned its name from the long calms which came upon its waters. But those calms were interspersed with sudden and violent storms. The harbors were poor and the channels of entrance unmarked. It was just the kind of a situation to discourage most men but to rouse the pioneering spirit of a man like William Wheelwright.

When five years had passed he went home, but not to stay. He had made up his mind to cast in his lot, for a time, with the South American leaders who were so eager to develop their newly independent countries. Within the year he was on the way back with his wife, Martha Bartlet of Newburyport, niece of the neighbor shipowner who had given him his commission as captain of the ill-fated *Rising Empire*. It took a brave woman to risk the adventure of South American journeying at that time, as Martha found out on the way to her new home. They had made the decision to try the Panama route instead of going the long way round by Cape Horn, but the crossing of the Isthmus by muleback proved to be a trip full of real hardships. One pauses often, as one seeks out the story of Wheelwright's life, to salute this New England girl who had the blood of seafaring, adventuring ancestors in her veins, as he had it in his. For the next forty-five years she followed his fortunes wherever they led, entering fully into his South American interests.

The news which met them at Guayaquil was of misfortune. The prosperous business which Wheelwright had left in the hands of a partner had been mismanaged, so that all his property had been lost. Instead of bringing his bride to a life of comfort and prosperity, he must start at the bottom again. This he decided to do in Valparaiso, thinking the opportunities better there. So now began the life in Chile, where he turned his energies beyond his own business and played an important part in the development of the country.

III

Valparaiso was a small seaport with a poor harbor and no modern improvements. The streets were ill paved; there was no water system, no street-lighting system, and little about the town would attract either business or immigration. But there was a beautiful location, with the possibility of a fine harbor, and the leaders in Chile were progressive and ambitious. Within a few years Wheelwright was to bring water works and a gas-lighting system and to persuade the officials to build a lighthouse at the harbor's entrance and provide better docks which would attract shipping.

There was probably little to distinguish this quiet, unassuming, friendly man from other merchants and sea captains, both British and American, who were in Chile in those days. But those who came to know him found that besides his trading trips by sea he was making exploring trips on horseback up and down the length of the narrow strip of land which is Chile. When he returned from these expeditions he could tell the people of their own resources, of the coal and saltpeter and borax and lime he had found, and of places where he thought new mines should be opened.

In 1835 he watched a severe earthquake wreck the lightly built houses and planned to set up brick kilns for the manufacture of bricks, from which heavier structures could be built. He came to know in the deserts the need for water. Workmen could not develop the resources that were there because they could not live on the barren sands. With the impulse that was always his to find out the remedy for any condition, he sent home to the United States for information about apparatus for distilling pure water from sea water. When the time came he was ready with such apparatus.

He was not a talkative man. Even his friends did not know of the idea that was growing in his mind. But when he had made his decision he began to discuss his plan. There could be no real gains, he had decided, without better ship service. The country was too isolated. There should be steamboats on the Pacific, serving the ports of the west coast as sailing vessels could not possibly do.

One has to try to put oneself back into that time, more than one hundred years ago, to know how tremendously progressive that idea was. It was only a year since the *Great Western*, a big wooden vessel driven by steam, had made its spectacular trip across the Atlantic, covering the distance in twelve days and bringing one hundred and fifty passengers. Indeed, Stephenson's railway, the first steam railway in England, had been running not more than ten years. Those things had happened in England, where the minds of the people had been prepared for such innovations. But this was the west coast of South America, distant one hundred and twenty days by sailing vessel from London. Our own Pacific coast was practically undeveloped. Gold had not yet been discovered in California. The Pacific was known chiefly as the route beyond Cape Horn to the Far East.

Yet Wheelwright was talking of steamboats on the Pacific, declaring that this ocean, with its calms and its currents, was particularly well fitted for this new kind of service. It was no wonder that people thought him crazy.

"Tell that insane Wheelwright that I am not at home. I am never at home to him," the British minister instructed his servant; and the boys in the streets, hearing the talk of their elders, hooted at the American as he went about his business.

But the British and American merchants began to be interested. Their home governments were discussing steam service to the West Indies. Probably it was due to come sometime, but they saw no hope for finding money for such an experiment.

Wheelwright went ahead as if there were no obstacles in his way. There is something breath-taking in the account of his patient, slow, methodical procedure. For steamboat service there must be government permission. So he went to the legislatures with his requests. If he got a steamboat service, would they grant him the necessary permission for the use of harbors, so that he could land his freight and passengers and have receiving ships for coaling? Would they grant him exclusive rights for the first ten years, so that the new line would have time to develop and pay its investors before rivals came into the field? It took him a couple of years to get these permissions. For the Bolivian rights he had to cross the Andes to get to Potosí, where the congress was meeting. He ran into a battle on the way and took down the last words of the defeated leader, who happened to be one of his friends, before he was executed by the victorious general. He had to go the whole length of the three-thousand-mile coast again and again in his little sixty-ton vessel, the *Fourth of July*. But at last he was on his way to London with the concessions in his pocket, and when, a little later, a group of British merchants in Argentina and Chile began to investigate the possibility of steam mail service to London, at the command of their government, they had to report back that nothing could be done independently, for Wheelwright had all the local rights. The Yankee had gotten ahead of them.

One would have liked to follow this New England sea captain about in London. He was forty years old at this time, a man of large build and dignified bearing, with a frank, open countenance and friendly, courteous manners. It took him months to win his point, and he was often utterly discouraged, as his letters to his Newburyport home show. But other reports show how he was making more progress than he thought. The Londoners liked him. Important officials, recently returned from South American trips, took him under their wing. He went as guest to a meeting of the Royal Geographical Society and was called on to speak. It was hardly fair, he wrote home, to call on him under such circumstances. But he acquitted himself well. No one who met him could fail to be impressed with his complete grasp of his subject. There was no question that they could ask him for which he did not have the answer.

The Britons were already carrying on a profitable trade with South America. They knew the wealth of natural products there. When Wheelwright talked of cutting the time between London and the west-coast ports in half, by a steamboat line on the Pacific, a journey across the narrow Isthmus, and a connection with a similar steamboat line between the West Indies and England, they listened with interest. To cut a trip that now took one hundred and twenty days to sixty days meant money to them.

So Wheelwright finally got his company, the Pacific Steam Navigation Company, with a capital of a quarter of a million pounds, with himself as superintendent, to shoulder all the responsibility and put the project through. He stayed in London to oversee the building of his two boats, the *Chile* and the *Peru*.

And this, we need to keep reminding ourselves, was only six years after the trip across the Atlantic of the *Great Western* and in the year when the first passenger line between the United States and Great Britain was being started.

IV

The Valparaiso newspapers pick up the story. On October 16, 1840, a salute fired by ships in the harbor announced the arrival of the *Chile* and the *Peru*. Four thousand people hurried up to the hills that overlooked the harbor to see the sight. Military bands went out on launches to greet them, playing their welcome. There was a stiff wind blowing, but every boat in the harbor, whether large or small, took on board all the passengers it could carry and set sail to get as near the steamboats as it could.

All [reads the record] were anxious to have a nearer view of these ponderous ships which moved without aid of sail or oar.

Both steamers crossed and recrossed the bay in different directions, receiving the salutations of the immense multitudes attracted by a spectacle altogether novel in these waters.

The great moment came when Wheelwright appeared on the quarterdeck of the *Chile*, on which he had journeyed from London. As he stood there, hat in hand, the bands played and the guns roared, while the crowds on the hills above the harbor "shouted their hurrahs to the energetic projector who had thus opened for the free States of the Pacific a new era of progress and prosperity."

Steam had come to the Pacific, but its "energetic projector," as the newspaper named him, had made only a beginning of his project. Hardly had the two steamers been welcomed in the southern and northern ports when an accident happened to the machinery of the *Chile*, and Wheelwright had to face the fact that there was no convenient repair shop at hand nor were there any docking facilities nearer than Guayaquil.

Then a more serious misfortune befell the undertaking. The coal which was due to come overland for the fueling of the ships failed to arrive, and for three long months the two steamboats lay idle in the harbors. But where was Wheelwright in the meantime? Far in the interior, prospecting for coal. Charles Darwin, on his South American trip, had seen samples of coal from the south of Chile and declared it of a quality useless for heavy fuel. The natives did not at this time require coal, for the easily obtained charcoal was sufficient for fires in that climate. But Wheelwright found valuable coal of excellent quality, thus uncovering one of Chile's richest future resources.

There were triumphs following the difficulties. To the North American mind the greatest was, perhaps, the one mentioned modestly by Wheelwright in a letter to one of his financial backers.

"I will just mention," Wheelwright writes, "that we have made trips along the coast, touching at ten ports, without varying a quarter of an hour from our schedule time."

That was a record which no transportation system of one hundred years later, whether by water, land, or air, can better.

But Wheelwright's two steamers, traveling back and forth between Guayaquil and Valparaiso in the year 1840, were only parts of a larger project. Ever since he had come to the west coast he had been interested in the Isthmus of Panama. He had been up there several times on personal exploring trips, trying to figure out the best route for a road, and later a railroad or canal, across this thirty-mile strip of land between the oceans.

"I was convinced," he writes, "that this route would become the highroad between the Pacific and the Atlantic."

In this conviction he was not alone. Soon after he

came to Guayaquil he had talked with an engineer whom General Bolívar had commissioned to make a survey of the region. He had searched the libraries and archives of Lima, Panama City, and Cartagena, in the hope of finding ancient Spanish records, but without result. Now in 1840, as soon as he had gotten his steamship service running, he went up there again, to make a further and more complete survey than any he had undertaken before.

The report of his journeys was printed in London in 1844, as he gave it that year before the Royal Geographical Society; and as we read the printed pages and look at the careful maps we add much to our picture of Wheelwright. Here is the scientist, taking soundings, measuring heights above sea level, studying the geological formation of the region, sinking experimental mining shafts for coal for his steamers, and recording his impressions of the natives.

There are the personal touches, too. One region was forbidden ground for any stranger and certainly for any white man. But Wheelwright accepted the invitation of the local Indian chief and went ashore with him in his canoe, leaving his companions behind to wait and worry until he returned. He went to the borders of that forbidden territory, got the information he needed as to the character of the land, and had a delightful visit in this aboriginal camp. He could but marvel, he reported on his return to the boat, at the hospitality, dignity, and courtesy of these simple people.

It was the rainy season when he was there, and he came out of the region suffering severely from fever contracted from exposure in the dense forests. But that was a mere incident of the trip, one like a dozen others on his exploring trips. There had been the time back in the mountains of Potosí, where he was investigating silver mines, when he and his party narrowly escaped being buried in a mountain pass by a snowslide. On that expedition his guides became so exhausted by climbing in the high altitude that, just before they reached the summit of the mountain, they declared themselves ready to lie down and die rather than go forward; and it was the North American Wheelwright who forced the stimulants which he fortunately had with him down their throats and got them sufficiently revived so that they were able to dig out an excavation in the snow within which they all, with their mules, could survive the night. Hints of such experiences may be found in the records of almost any one of these exploring trips, but to him they were evidently part of the day's work and hardly worth the mentioning.

Wheelwright did not build the Panama road nor the railroad which followed it, though he wanted to do so. But of one thing we may be very sure. It was his line of steamers, with the service which he succeeded in 1845 in extending up the west coast to Panama, which made those roads necessary. It was he that focused the attention on the importance of Panama and created the need for an easy means of transportation across the Isthmus.

If one doubts it, read the delightful prospectus, or "letter," which he addressed to the public, through the columns of the London *Morning Post* in 1844, and reflect as you read it that there was not yet a railroad from sea to sea. This event which he was announcing was simply a monthly steam service between Panama and the west-coast ports, though his four steamboats were to connect with steamers carrying the royal mail from London to the West Indies. Yet, as surely as the builders of the Panama Canal, he was seeing the Isthmus as the highway to the Far East. Here is part of the "letter":

I have thought it well to make this announcement that it may be transmitted to Australia, New Zealand, and the islands which form the Eastern Archipelago, in order that the residents of these remote countries may be prepared to take immediate advantage of the intercourse now existing between them *and the western coast of America*, which will open to them a new and expeditious route.

The inauguration of the proposed line will undoubtedly

also attract the attention of many who have occasion to visit China.

V

To us of the United States, whose territory was opened up so differently, Wheelwright's order of procedure comes as a surprise. Yet it is justified by its success. Still, one can but feel that only a man of extraordinary vision could have looked over the entire field and laid out his plans so wisely.

The ocean was the highway of travel; hence, the steamboats came first. Then there must be harbors, and all the undertakings in Chile followed the inauguration of steamboat service: the improvements in the city of Valparaiso, the building of lighthouses, the development of the harbor. All these things he had planned, and now he carried them out.

Then he was ready for the third step: railways, beginning with short railways from inland mines to the coast. There is another amazing tale here, of the way he persuaded a whole town, that of Copiapó, to move to a better location while he was building a railway in place of an impassable wagon road, to make their rich copper and silver mines, ninety miles inland, accessible.

Lastly, he had in mind that which should fulfill his dream of uniting east and west as well as north and south—a transcontinental railway. In 1855 he withdrew from all connection with the steamship company and turned his entire attention to the financing and building of railways.

One could begin a whole new story from the letters which tell of his sending groups of surveyors and engineers up into the Andes to find out the best route and then going himself on horseback over the entire distance to make sure of its being the best way. He wanted to begin in Chile and work eastward, but the Chilean government rejected his proposal. So we have him returning, thirty and more years after his arrival there, to Buenos Aires, to lay out his plans for a railway which should start at the east coast and move westward.

There had been great changes in those thirty years. The need of railways between the growing cities was recognized. But there were rivals now, other companies seeking to embrace the opportunity. There were political difficulties as well, causing lengthy delays, revolutions, and counter-revolutions. In 1863, however, Wheelwright had the satisfaction of seeing the Grand Central Argentine Railway, of his creation, started at Rosario, on the Paraná River, and carried during seven long years across the pampas to the far inland city of Cordoba, hundreds of miles in the interior. By this time the telegraph had been invented, and he was able to add that instrument of communication along his railroad lines.

In his speech at the opening of that railroad he gave the people a vision of what such a railway, when carried across the continent, would accomplish.

"It will bring together," he said, "and unite the great South American family of nations by new sympathies; it will open up new commercial developments; it will discover new merchandise, new interchanges of products; it will make South America the steppingstone between Europe and Australia, that vast future empire of the West; it will strengthen the South American states and enable them to concentrate against invasion."

Prophetic words those, to have been spoken in 1863!

The South American story of William Wheelwright ends with the building of a short railroad from Buenos Aires to a better port of his selection, near the site of his shipwreck in the Plata Bay fifty years earlier, and his journey to England and death in London in that same year of 1873. But for our story there is a New England postscript.

Wheelwright had always kept in close touch with his family and his Newburyport home, intending to return there for his last years. That was denied him, but when his will was read it was found that he had desired to have his body taken to his birthplace for burial in the family plot and that he had left a considerable portion of his property for the establishment of a fund for the scientific education of boys of Newburyport. That fund is still carrying on his purpose, sending boys to institutions of higher education. So he has a living memorial in New England, matching the high honors paid him in South America.

Henry Meiggs, Promoter and Railroad Builder

"ANYWHERE A LLAMA GOES, I CAN TAKE A TRAIN."—*Meiggs*

ON AN OCTOBER NIGHT IN THE YEAR 1854
the barque *America* slipped silently, under cover of
darkness, out of San Francisco Bay and headed south. It
had come into the harbor loaded with piles of sweet-
smelling lumber from the Oregon forests and had been
due to go back for more. The ships of Henry Meiggs's
lumber fleet could not bring building materials fast
enough for the rapidly growing city, only six years

away from the gold rush which had started a stream of Easterners to California. This time the *America* was carrying furniture, household articles, and all the personal effects of a family, as if it were a moving van, and was bound for a distant South American port. These things had been brought to the dock hastily, in the hours following midnight; and as hastily and stealthily there came aboard, at the turn of the tide, five passengers: Henry Meiggs, the ship's owner, and his wife and their three children.

They came from a party, a party which would be talked of in San Francisco for many a day. Every window of the fine Meiggs mansion had been brilliantly lighted, and the onlookers who gathered on the street watched the *elite* of San Francisco, society folk and city officials, arrive in their carriages. Mr. Meiggs liked to give such parties, and who had a better right? He had helped to build the city and was a leader in all the projects for its development. Everyone liked "Honest Harry Meiggs," as they called him. He was a fine-looking man, tall and with an imposing manner, yet cordial and friendly with all, whether they were rich or poor. Through the windows he could be seen receiving his guests with cheerful face and moving about and talking and laughing with one and another, to make them feel at home. There was no sign of his secret knowledge that within a few hours the mansion would be emptied and he would be on his way to South America.

The ship was far out to sea when the news broke the next day that "Honest Harry" had been caught in the business slump which was following the "gold-rush boom" and had been tempted into borrowing half a million dollars of city money on forged warrants, as well as money entrusted to him by investors, in a vain attempt to save his credit. It is a sign of how far South America was, in those days, from the United States, especially on the Pacific coast, that there was no thought of pursuing him and bringing him back. He had gone, and that was all there was to it. There was no telegraph, no mail service, no port-to-port service.

Years were to pass before occasional travelers, going south, were to bring back reports of Meiggs's spectacular successes in Chile and Peru. Then money payments began to come back, giving a hint of what may have been in his mind when he went out to seek a new life in a new land. He was not the first man to use one of the Americas as a place of escape after efforts to get rich too quickly, nor to turn the money gained back in an attempt at restitution.

South America gained by Meiggs's coming. The same qualities of vision and daring which had brought him to California at the first call of the gold rush and made him a leader in the development of that new region were to make him useful in the new projects which were being undertaken there.

Henry Meiggs had been born in Catskill, New York, in 1811, and had gone into the lumber business, first in small towns in New York State and then in New York City. He had always been venturesome in business and had failed in the panic of 1837 and again in 1842. Then in 1848 he had sailed out of New York harbor with a cargo of lumber and had brought it around South America by Cape Horn to San Francisco. He had sold it at an enormous profit and then had made his shrewd move. While others were rushing to the gold mines, staking their claims and prospecting, he was building sawmills and sending his men all up and down the coast into the uncut forests for lumber, so that he could have building materials on hand for the needs of the growing city. In the next years he doubled and tripled his money in this business.

But he was more than a successful businessman. In the strange "boom town," with its shifting population and its many problems, he was a pillar of strength. There was need of a pier for the increasing shipping, and he built a very long one out into the harbor. He had been a patron of the arts in New York, president of a musical society and giving generously to its support. Now he built for San Francisco an imposing music hall, at a time when most people were not looking beyond the needs of the present day for food and shelter. He was elected a supervisor of the county and a member of the board of aldermen, and in that office got the contract for planking the city's streets with his lumber. It was in this deal that he overreached himself and dipped into the city treasury to meet his obligations when the end of the boom caused bankers to call in their loans. Then he was off to Chile, preferring exile to the facing of failure and disgrace.

In Chile he found conditions just to his liking. Here, too, there was talk of big enterprises and rapid development of the country. The government officials were starting to build railroads. Wheelwright had built a short one from the mines to the coast and had urged the laying out of others, but the men had not been ready. Now they were undertaking the construction of the Valparaiso-to-Santiago road which Wheelwright had suggested and were already having troubles. Meiggs began modestly enough as construction superintendent on certain stretches of the line, becoming, meanwhile, acquainted with the men in charge and familiar with the problems of railroad building. Several contractors had already been ruined, having failed to calculate the costs rightly, and had poured out all their money without getting the promised results. At the critical moment Meiggs stepped forward and offered to finish the railroad for $12,000,000, and the government accepted his offer. He was to have four years to do it, but he finished it in less than two, winning for himself a spectacular reputation—and a personal profit of well over a million dollars. It was characteristic of him that he promptly put five hundred thousand dollars of this money into a fine house for himself and his family at Santiago, Chile's capital city.

That was the beginning of a series of astonishing and successful ventures, which won him his fame. If he had been only a promoter, he would have been soon forgotten in spite of his financial profits. But he promoted undertakings which were worth while, projects that others had undertaken and abandoned or had not dared to undertake, and managed by one means or another to carry them through. Within a few years he had built other roads, getting the contracts from Chilean and Peruvian legislators by resort to every means from persuasion to bribery, and had achieved a reputation as a man who could achieve the impossible in engineering feats.

Then the time came, in the late 1860s, when the Peruvian government desired to open up the vast mineral wealth beyond the Andes by constructing a railroad across, through, or around them. European engineers scoffed at the project as impossible. They declared that even a narrow-gauge road, with toothed wheels fitting into notched rails, was utterly impracticable at these dizzy heights. The American said that he would construct a standard-gauge road, of the usual cross-country type, on which ordinary trains would run without the use of a single cogwheel or cable. But it would cost $125,000,000 in gold. He was questioned and challenged in the Peruvian legislature, but nothing could shake his calm and confident stand.

"Anywhere a llama goes, I can take a train," he declared, and at last they believed him and gave him the contract.

The result is the Callao-Lima-Oroya Railroad, the highest in the world, and to this day and perhaps for all time the most remarkable feat of railroad engineering, for in the future mountain heights are more likely to be surmounted by ships soaring in the air than by trains crawling upward on steel rails. The Santiagans had called his five-hundred-thousand-dollar mansion "Meiggs' Folly," but now they could so describe almost every section of the road while it was in the building, for none could believe that the task he had set himself could be accomplished.

In the midst of all the talking and doubting and ridi-

culing, Meiggs went calmly ahead. When the first section of the road was finished to Arequipa in southern
Peru, a city well over a mile and a half above sea level,
Meiggs celebrated the achievement by an entertainment
which was attended by the Peruvian president and two
thousand guests, an entertainment which lasted for two
weeks and cost him two hundred thousand dollars of
his own money. But the great task was still ahead of him.
He had come across deserts of shifting sands, where
wagon roads had been impracticable and his materials
and equipment had been brought in along mule tracks.
Now he came to solid rock, through which he must cut
or around and over which he must lay his rails.

The road must be seen and traveled for any realiza-
tion of its wonders. Yet one can get something of the
picture by piling up figures: sixty-seven tunnels, the
highest of them through the mountain which was named
for him, Mount Meiggs, being at an altitude only 136
feet under the height of the summit of Mont Blanc in
Switzerland; the first use of the so-called "switchback"
or zigzag system of railroading in the New World, with
the rails laid across mountain walls such as had never
before been surmounted, so that at one place one can
look from the train both upward and downward and
see five sections of the road, already crossed below or to
be traveled above. Meiggs came to a place where a river

was in his way, and he turned its water into a tunnel of his making and used the river bed for his tracks. The actual construction was a feat of unexampled human endurance. In one place engineers and men had to be swung across a mountain gorge on wire ropes, suspended some hundred or more feet in the air between two cliffs. Again and again workmen had to be lowered by ropes and held by ropes as they cut out the footholds and standing places for beginning their work.

Nowadays the trains carry oxygen tanks for those who cannot stand the altitude, and passengers are cautioned against exerting themselves by walking about or moving quickly at the stops. These workmen had to spend hours laboring at these altitudes, with danger always of the painful and dangerous mountain sickness, *soroche*, with its congestion of the lungs. Henry Meiggs and his brother John, whom he brought from the United States to take charge of the work, paid every attention to the well-being of their workmen, but in spite of all they could do, there was a high percentage of deaths, both from the conditions of the work and from malignant fever which swept through the camps.

Meiggs had contracted for his huge payments of gold at every stage of the job. But the money in the Peruvian treasury gave out, and he advanced from his own funds, until it was said at one time that he practically owned the republic. The bankers in Europe and England who were helping to finance the project lost faith and refused to pour in more funds. Meiggs put in the last dollar of his own private fortune to pay the overdue wages of his workmen. But still the work went on.

He did not live to see it completed, though the main part of the line was done. A war between Peru and Chile hindered its later completion, until in 1884 the contract was taken up by another firm of railroad builders. But it was he who tunneled through the mountain that bears his name and brought his road out on the other side of the great mountain barrier. To him belongs the glory of "breaking the backbone of the Andes."

Meiggs died in 1877, in the midst of his work and without ever returning to San Francisco. Through his friends it had been suggested again and again, doubtless by his desire, that an act be passed in the California legislature giving him immunity from punishment in case of his return. But although he had refunded the money he had taken, both to the government and to his creditors, that act was never passed. There are pleasant tales of the return of that money. One by one, as his fortunes prospered, his debts were wiped out, with interest for the years of his indebtedness. A washerwoman, to whom he had owed a few dollars at the time of his flight, was sought out by his men and given the payment for the bill and enough gold in addition to make her comfortable for life. Former acquaintances who looked him up in Peru in his later years returned with tales of a cordial welcome and lavish entertainment.

But it was in Chile and Peru that Henry Meiggs was beloved by the people. He had achieved for them the impossible in the speedy development of their countries, and they were profiting daily by his daring undertakings. In spite of his faults, they admired tremendously this impetuous, generous, energetic North American.

Young Darwin
in South America

"THE MAP OF THE WORLD CEASED TO BE
A BLANK."—*Charles Darwin*

SOUTH AMERICA HAS ALWAYS DRAWN
scientists from other parts of the world to seek out its
natural treasures. Here there are tropics and mountain
heights, prehistoric ruins and volcanoes in the making,
jungles and plains, with an endless variety of plant and
animal life. Alexander von Humboldt went out there
near the end of the days of Spanish rule and made
scientific discoveries which brought the continent to

the attention of Europe as no other man had done. But we are likely to forget the part which South America played in the life of Charles Darwin, who went there in 1832 when he was only twenty-two years old, and the contribution he made to South America by his report of his life there. His famous book, *The Voyage of the Beagle,* became a best seller in his own time and has been printed and reprinted for all the hundred years since. No one can ever judge the effect of a book like that on people who are considering a trip to a somewhat unknown country or thinking of doing business or settling there.

Our interest in Darwin's trip is that he saw pioneer conditions, as young Wheelwright saw them, at the time when the modern republics were beginning. He came to the continent eight years after the final battle of the Wars of Independence. He tells, as any young man just out of college might tell, of his travels in a country not unlike our own Middle and Far West in their pioneer days. We get close to South America as we follow him around and see its people—not the famous leaders, but the ordinary Americans who were going to build the new, independent nations, as our own people created new Western states.

No one was ever more glad to get ashore and stay ashore, after a long Atlantic voyage, than young Dar-

win. He had not known, until England was left behind,
how much he was going to suffer from seasickness; and
for anyone who did, life in a small sailing vessel like
the *Beagle* was sheer discomfort for a good portion of
the time. The expedition was for the surveying of the
waters off the southern and eastern coasts of South
America and other areas of water and coast in the
Pacific, and Charles Darwin had thought himself ex-
tremely lucky to get the chance to go along as naturalist. His shipmates tell how plucky he was about his
seasickness. He had a hammock slung next to his bench
on the deck and would stop his work on his precious
specimens of sea plants and animals and lie down for a
few minutes when the roll of the boat became too much
for him and then get up and go to work again.

So when the ship came to the shores of Brazil, and
he had the excellent errand of needing to see and study
the tropical plants and trees, he was only too thankful
to spend some time on land. Almost as soon as he came
ashore he had a chance to have a day in a tropical forest,
and because he was a naturalist, trained to observe, he
gives us more feeling of it than does almost anyone else
of that time. "The elegance of the grasses," he says, "the
novelty of the parasitical plants, the beauty of the flowers, the glossy green of the foliage, but above all the
general luxuriance of the vegetation, filled me with ad-

miration." To be in such a forest was the most exciting thing that had ever happened to him. He was amazed at the noise made by the insects, which was so loud that it might be heard even in a vessel anchored several hundred yards from shore. Yet when he went farther into the recesses of the forest a universal silence appeared to reign. The tall trees, almost smothered along their lower trunks by orchid-bearing plants, were a marvel to him, as were the conical ants' nests nearly twelve feet high. Could anything be more thrilling to a youth who had never before been outside of England than to be taken by a Portuguese priest for a day's hunting of—what?— monkeys, parrots, and toucans?

The next trip inland was farther south, from Montevideo, along the Uruguay River, on the Banda Oriental, or "east bank," as Uruguay was then called. This was a horseback trip into cattle country, and he was surprised at the primitive conditions of life. These people who entertained him so hospitably owned great *estancias*, or ranches, with thousands of cattle. Yet his host lived in a miserable house, with a floor of hardened mud and windows without glass. The supper, served for quite a company, was only beef, roast or boiled as one chose, with some pieces of pumpkin and no bread, while the land around the house would have grown any vegetable.

The young English naturalist was a source of per-

petual astonishment to the people. The whole family
gathered to see him strike a match. They had never
seen fire made that way before. "In every house," he
says, "I was asked to show the compass, and by its aid,
together with a map, to point out the direction of various places. It excited the liveliest admiration that I, a
perfect stranger, should know the road (for 'direction'
and 'road' are synonymous in this open country) to
places where I had never been."

Here he had his first acquaintance with Gauchos,
those picturesque cattlemen who were like our cowboys
of the Western ranches, yet different. At a drinking
shop he met a considerable number of them, who had
been out with their cattle all day. Tall, handsome, proud
of manner, with long mustaches, and black hair curling
down their backs, they were dressed in brightly colored
garments, with great spurs clanking at their heels when
they moved. They made him graceful bows and treated
him with the utmost politeness. But he looked at the
knives stuck as daggers at their waists and, remembering
the tales he had heard, felt sure that, if occasion arose,
they would as readily cut a stranger's throat as make
graceful bows to him. The independence of their life
fascinated him. To a university student, who had never
in his life spent a night in the open, there was a great
appeal in their freedom. "To be able at any moment to

pull up your horse and say, 'Here we will pass the night,'" needing only to find in the neighborhood the four essentials of life—pasture for the horses, water, meat, and firewood—that was surely to owe no man, and no town, anything.

He stopped near the camp of General Rosas, an Argentinean who was on his way to be military dictator of the country, and saw what manner of man was equal to ruling these Gauchos. The story was told to him of the way of choosing a general from among them when an army had been assembled. A troop of unbroken horses was herded into a corral, which had a gateway on one side with a high crossbar above it on which a man could perch. Here candidates for the office went and took their turn, while the men watched. A wild horse was let out through the gateway, and the man who could drop on his back and ride him without saddle or bridle, and then bring him back to the door of the corral, was their general. Rosas had performed this feat, and the Gauchos worshiped him for this and other signs of his power.

Darwin came to be quite a horseman himself as he went up and down the land in search of strange birds, animals, insects, and plants. His journal mentions a four-hundred-mile journey on horseback and then a three-hundred-mile expedition across the pampas. Before he left the east coast of South America to make the long voyage around the southern part of the continent, the young naturalist had become a veteran camper. But who of the Gauchos or gentlemen owners of estates who showed hospitality to this pleasant young man and answered his innumerable questions could have suspected that there was forming in his mind a theory as to the origin of all living things which was to change the thinking of the scientific world? Least of all, probably, Darwin himself, for he was a modest youth.

Fortune favored him in Chile, though it was a sad fortune which he never would have wished for his kindly hosts. Everywhere he was studying the structure of the earth and trying to picture by what kind of gigantic cataclysms the huge mountain ranges had been formed. As he visited places along the coast he was excited to see seashells embedded in rocks two and three hundred feet above the sea. Such land had evidently been thrown up within fairly recent times, as geologic time was measured. Then on February 20, 1835, there came one of the most severe earthquakes ever experienced in Chile, a shock that covered a space seven hundred miles in one line and four hundred in another.

At first his attention was wholly taken up by sympathy for the misery of the people. At Concepción he saw the whole coast strewed over with timber and fur-

niture, as if a thousand ships had been wrecked. The
ruined towns, with hardly a house left standing, were
a "most awful, yet interesting spectacle." With vivid
imagination he tried to picture what would happen in
his own country if such an event occurred.

Earthquakes [he wrote] are sufficient to destroy the
prosperity of any country. If beneath England the now
inert subterranean forces should exert those powers . . .
how completely would the entire condition of the country
be changed! What would become of the lofty houses,
thickly packed cities, great manufactories? . . . In every
large town famine would go forth, pestilence and death
following in its train.

Yet what excited him as a geologist was to see the
very earth-building events which he had been trying to
picture happening almost before his eyes. He saw islands
that had been lifted, in that moment of shock, five, ten,
twelve feet. He found damp, living sea creatures clinging to rocks far above sea level. An island with which
he was familiar was lessened in size to an extent which,
in his judgment, it would have taken the ordinary wear
and tear of the sea and the weather a full hundred years
to accomplish. Now he could read a definite meaning
into seashells which he was shown 600 feet, 1000 feet,
and even 1300 feet above the shore line. He had seen a
continent in the making. He had had visible proof of

his growing theory that the changes which threw one set of rocks up and lowered another ridge were not necessarily a single, terrific cataclysm of the far-distant past, but a series of uprisings, repeated over long periods of time. His crowning proof was to come, but already he had seen enough to lay the foundation of his theory.

Now he must go up into the mountains, even though it would be an expensive trip, such as he hesitated to afford. The expedition must be off at once, if he was to go, for with the end of March the Chilean summer (exact opposite, by dates, of our season) would be nearing its end, and there would be danger of being overtaken by snow in the high passes. He must take, he was told, a guide and a muleteer, with ten mules and a *madrina*. What, he inquired, was a *madrina*, and why must he take one?

The *madrina* (or godmother) is a most important personage [he wrote in his journal]; she is an old steady mare, with a little bell around her neck; and wherever she goes, the mules, like good children, follow her. The affection of these animals for their *madrinas* saves infinite trouble. If several large troops are turned into one field to graze, in the morning the muleteers have only to lead the *madrinas* a little apart and tinkle their bells; although there may be two or three hundred together, each mule immediately knows the bell of its own *madrina* and comes to her. . . .

In a troop each animal carries on a level road a cargo

weighing 416 pounds, but in a mountainous country one hundred pounds less; yet with what delicate limbs, without proportional bulk of muscle, these animals support so great a burden!

Four of the ten mules used on this trip carried cargoes, the others being used for riding; and there was frequent "turn and turn about," so that each should perform both services. Darwin wrote to his sister that he traveled on this trip in uncommon comfort, having a bed (probably a mattress that could be rolled up and slung on the back of one of the animals) instead of sleeping on the bare ground.

The pictures he gives of Chilean life are interesting. He went up through green, fertile valleys, with orchards of apple, nectarine, and peach trees loaded with fruit, and came to more bleak and barren regions, where he met herds of cattle being driven down from the high valleys before winter overtook them. Much farther up, almost at the top of the ridge, he met a large party making the Transandine crossing with goods and supplies on seventy loaded mules. "It was interesting," he wrote, "to hear the wild cries of the muleteers and to watch the long descending strings of the animals; they appeared so diminutive, there being nothing but the black mountains with which they could be compared."

The manner of traveling was delightfully independent. In the inhabited parts they bought a little firewood, hired pasture for the animals, and bivouacked in the corner of the same field with them. Carrying an iron pot, they cooked and ate their supper under a cloudless sky, and Darwin was happy. There is a tale about that pot when they got to the top of the pass. Because of the altitude, the water boiled at a lower temperature than it would have in the villages below. The guide and the muleteer found the potatoes hard after some hours of boiling and left the pot on the fire all night. But still the potatoes were uncooked. Darwin heard them talking the matter over and blaming the "cursed pot." It was a new one, they said, and "did not choose to boil potatoes."

These mountains were rich in ores, and the guide told stories of the discovery of some of the richest mines. In these barren regions men searched every slope for firewood, and every Chilean laborer learned to recognize the most familiar minerals. By such men, hunting for wood or for their lost mules, nearly all the richest mines had been discovered.

Chanuncillo [wrote Darwin], from which silver to the value of many hundred thousand pounds has been raised in the course of a few years, was discovered by a man who threw a stone at his loaded donkey and, thinking that it was very heavy, picked it up again and found it full of pure silver: the vein occurred at no great distance, standing up like a wedge of metal.

The mountain pass by which he was crossing was one of the six used by General San Martín's troops ten years before, as they crossed by several routes in order to surprise the Spanish army. As the party came nearer the heights, some twelve thousand feet above sea level, the mules halted every fifty yards and then, after resting a few seconds, started on again of their own accord. He himself found little discomfort, even at this altitude, and what little he did have was completely forgotten when he made his thrilling discovery, the story of which everyone who knows the work of Charles Darwin remembers. At that mountain height, higher than most of the mountains of Switzerland, he found a group of fossil seashells embedded in the rocks. His surmise was proved. There could be no doubt any longer. These loftiest of mountains had been pushed up from a great depth in some prehistoric time. The joy of the discovery kept him from needing any other stimulant, in spite of the lack of oxygen in the air. "I literally could hardly sleep at night," he wrote home to his sister, "for thinking over my day's work."

No one could cross these mountains unmoved by a sense of awe. "When we reached the crest and looked backward," he wrote, "a glorious view was presented.

The atmosphere resplendently clear; the sky an intense blue; the profound valleys; the wild, broken forms; the heaps of ruins, piled up during the lapse of ages; the bright-colored rocks, contrasted with the quiet mountains of snow: all these together produced a scene no one could have imagined. Neither plant nor bird, excepting a few condors wheeling around the higher pinnacles, distracted my attention from the inanimate mass. I felt glad that I was alone: it was like watching a thunderstorm or hearing in full orchestra a chorus of the *Messiah*."

The return journey was over the Uspallata Pass, and Darwin was back in the home of friends in Santiago after a remarkable twenty-two-day expedition. Once more he chose to make a hard land journey through the mining regions and deserts of northern Chile rather than going to Peru by water on the *Beagle*. This was country he wished to see and examine carefully, in spite of the hardships of the trip.

His first goal was Copiapó, an important mining center more than four hundred miles to the north, in the region where William Wheelwright was prospecting at this very period and planning to build his first railroad, for the purpose of bringing out the copper and other minerals from the mines to the port of Caldera. Darwin was interested in the miners, who descended 450 feet into the earth and brought up, on each trip, 200 pounds' weight of stone, climbing by footholds cut ladderlike into trees placed slanting to make a zigzag path on the sides of the open shaft. He tells of their costume, "peculiar and rather picturesque," a very long, dark-colored shirt with an apron, a bright-colored sash, broad trousers, and a small cap of scarlet. The natives could not understand this eager young foreigner. If he had been hunting for mines, like other prospectors! But he did not seem to care any more about deposits of minerals than about plants or ordinary rocks, and he asked so many questions about earthquakes and changes in the height of lakes and volcanoes. Darwin asked them if they, too, were not curious about the reasons for earthquakes and volcanoes, and hot springs and cold, and rainy seasons and dry. They shook their heads. Those were things no one knew.

It was a varied experience Darwin had, of going from sea voyaging to mountain climbing, and from the forests and jungles of Brazil's riverbanks, and the grassy plains of Argentina, to the deserts of Chile. In the middle of May, when he was at the town of Coquimbo on the coast, it rained lightly for about five hours. He was told that the farmers would hurry to break up the ground at once, in order to take advantage of this moisture. When a second shower came they would plant seed. If there should be a third, their harvest would be assured.

From this part of Chile, Darwin went north on the *Beagle* to Peru, which he found in a sad condition because of the feuds of would-be rulers, elected or gaining their authority by revolution. The pictures which he gives of the run-down condition of the city of Lima and the seaport of Callao show the need of the impetus soon to be given by steamships and railroad building.

The *Beagle* went on now to the Galápagos Islands, New Zealand, Australia, and came back by way of Pacific islands, and around the Cape of Good Hope for a stop in Brazil. Darwin was impressed by the horrors of slavery, as he saw it practiced there. On August 19, 1836, the ship left Brazil; on October 2 it landed in Falmouth, England. Darwin had been away from home for five years.

He had gone a student, barely out of the university. For those five years he had been sending home his specimens—plants, animal life, fossils, shells, minerals—with reports of their collection in the far parts of the world, and now he returned to find himself, at twenty-seven, recognized as one of the leading scientific men of England. Besides all this, there was his personal reward, which he was to share with others in his book, *The Voyage of the Beagle.*

From such a journey "the map of the world ceases to be a blank; it becomes a picture full of the most varied and animated figures. . . . Africa, or North and South America, are well-sounding names, and easily pronounced; but it is not until having sailed for weeks along small portions of their shores, that one is thoroughly convinced what vast spaces on our immense world these names imply. From seeing the present state, it is impossible not to look forward with high expectations to the future progress of nearly an entire hemisphere."

Hidden Treasure

A SEARCH THAT HAS LASTED UNTIL OUR OWN TIME

ONE WOULD THINK THAT THE SEARCH
for Indian treasure troves of gold would have ended
with the El Dorado story, but it seems that it will never
end. Back in the days of the conquest of Peru by the
Spaniards, there was gold hidden by the Indians to keep
it from the grasping hands of the invaders. To this day
there are tales of such stores of wealth in many parts
of the ancient Inca kingdom, and of them all none has

persisted more strongly than the story of a treasure trove buried beneath Mount Tunguragua, on the eastern edge of the Andes back of Ecuador. Here is the way it runs, with the tale of a botanist pioneer from England, who had found much treasure in South American plants before he followed this trail of gold.

Early in the nineteenth century, not much more than a hundred years ago, a Spaniard who had always been poor married an Indian girl, a native. He went with her to live near her father's home in the mountains back of Ecuador. Then, all at once, after a few years, he reappeared in Quito, bringing his wife with him and renting a fine house in which they began to live expensively. Such a change of fortune might have gone without much notice if it had not been noised about, after a considerable time, that this man by the name of Valverde deposited with his banker each month a cube of gold which looked as though it had come recently from the foundry.

That meant, to those who heard it, a gold mine somewhere, a secret mine, of which only the Indians knew. Perhaps it was one of the old Inca mines which was being worked again. Single nuggets of gold were frequently brought in by Indians from the hills, but this monthly delivery at the bank of a cube of always the same size—worth, some said, about $10,000—looked like more than a chance find. Neither Valverde nor his Indian wife explained where their money came from. The people of Quito could only look on and watch them spend it lavishly, without any apparent doubt of a continuous supply.

For a time the life in Quito satisfied the couple, and then Valverde departed for Spain, where he repeated his lavish spending, still with no word concerning its source. In a few years he died, leaving a sealed letter for the king of Spain, with a package containing a large number of these same gold cubes. Within that envelope was his will, leaving the treasure trove on which he had been drawing in distant Ecuador to the king, and with it a map accompanied by detailed instructions as to its location and the way to find it.

How do we know? you ask. Is not this one more legend, handed down by Indians or told to believing foreigners? That was the question that Richard Spruce, the famous English botanist, asked. He was in and out of South America for fifteen years, from 1849 to 1864. In that time he traveled up and down the northern half of the continent, studying and collecting its plants. During the period he actually sent home seven thousand flowering plants to be classified, making a tremendous contribution of knowledge of South American species, as well as adding to the information, both in the New

World and in the Old, concerning the regions he visited and searched so painstakingly.

Richard Spruce got to know the South Americans well, being made welcome in private homes in the countries where he made his long stays. When he came in the course of his wanderings to the region of the Llanganati, the most unknown part of Ecuador, he was told by friends that these mountains abounded in metals and that somewhere up near Tunguragua, one of the lofty volcanoes, there was an artificial lake, a lost lake, in which the Incas had deposited immense quantities of gold. They had done this back in Pizarro's time, so the story went, when the Inca Atahualpa had been taken prisoner and a ransom of gold had been demanded which should fill a twelve-foot-square room up to a certain height on the wall. Runners had been dispatched by the unfortunate emperor over the entire kingdom, telling his subjects to supply the needed gold. The word had come to this northerly and remote part of the kingdom, in the volcanic mountains that separated the western country from the Amazon forests on the other side. There they had collected their gold, bringing it by runners along the steep paths and the hanging bridges. But they were far, very far away. Long before they got their gold on the road, the room had been filled from other parts of the empire, and as they carried it southward they were met by the news that Atahualpa had been put to death by the conquering Spaniards.

Then it was that they made their lake, by turning mountain waters from their channel, and dropped that gold into it; and there, Richard Spruce was told, it had remained until this day, for the secret of its hiding place was lost. But there was the tale, too, of Señor Valverde, and his fortune, and his map making, not more than thirty years before. If Spruce was doubtful of it, he could see the map, for it was owned, or an exact copy of it was owned, by a Señor Salvador Ortega. He questioned further, and this gentleman graciously sent his copy for the Englishman's inspection.

Here were eight small sheets of paper which, when put together, made a map nearly four feet long by two feet, nine inches wide, accompanied by the *Derrotero*, or Guide, which the king of Spain had sent to the proper officials, after Valverde's death, with a "Royal Warrant" to go and find the treasure, of which the Spaniard had learned from his Indian wife and her father, descendant of the Indian chiefs who buried it. As soon as these instructions had been received, an expedition had been organized and had set out for the mountains, accompanied by a friar, Padre Longo, who knew the region well. But when they had arrived at the general locality and were trying to locate the places marked, the friar had disappeared, and no trace was ever found of him. He had probably fallen over some precipice or into some deep crevasse. But it was strange, was it not? Could it have been that the gold was not to be found?

Since then many people had seen the map in the archives of the town of Tacunga, and many attempts had been made to find the spot. But none had succeeded.

Richard Spruce was fascinated with the story and with the map and the directions as he read them. By his own knowledge of the region he could identify many of the places. There was no question in his mind, or that of others who had examined the map, that it had been drawn by one who had been often in these mountains.

He found men who had been on this first expedition of search, and they explained that when they got to a certain point there was fresh lava from the volcano, or so they thought, which had changed the appearance of the region. Spruce translated the documents into English and got a charter from the king of Spain to take up the search, as many had done before him. Those directions are in Quito now and are reprinted in the book which he published years later in England, describing all his researches.

They tell of the spot where the horses must be left, because one must next proceed afoot. They give the names of the mountains to be seen from this spot and the position of other landmarks. Then comes a five-day journey, with the path identified by this lake and that ravine, by a waterfall, a bridge of three poles, a hut for sleeping, another ravine, a mountain to be gone around, until at last the searcher comes to the "Way of the Inca," from which can be seen the entrance to the tunnel, "in the form of a church porch." Beyond the tunnel, when one has gone through, may be seen the cascade. In the bog will be noticed grains of gold. One is to leave the bog and ascend the mountain. If the mouth of the tunnel is closed by a certain growing plant, one is to remove the plant and discover the entrance. On the left-hand side one will see the *guayra*, the furnace for smelting.

It reads as if one could walk straight to it. But the distance covered in those five days was to be ninety miles, or thereabouts, as the searchers found. The region is one of sudden and violent floods in the mountain streams, and inactive volcanoes are suddenly noticed to be sending up thin lines of black smoke from hidden craters near their summits.

Richard Spruce took his party in and searched in vain, as others have searched since. The reports of the different trips have been left in Quito. No one doubts that the gold is there. But there is no doubt, either, that the changes of a hundred years have removed the landmarks and filled in the artificial lake, made four hundred years ago. Perhaps in Valverde's time the Indians of the high valley reached the store of treasure through this tunnel which the map describes. Perhaps there was a fresh mine, which was being worked.

The answer of the simple Indians who live in the region is sure. The mountain has hidden this Inca gold and is protecting it. The people gave it into the care of the mountain, and there it will remain.

But men will keep on searching, and in the search will be yielded the secrets of other metals. That is what the treasure hunts of South America have always brought forth. By such means, from the earliest days even to the present, the different regions have been opened up. Those who hunted along the Amazon found not yellow gold but the "white gold" of rubber. The silver mines of Bolivia led the way to the great tin deposits, which are one of the world's chief sources. The mountain regions of Colombia and the valley of the Orinoco have produced the "black gold" of oil.

Santos-Dumont, Brazil's Hero of the Air

**BRAZIL BECAME AIR-MINDED EARLY BE-
CAUSE OF ITS OWN AIRMAN, ITS FAMOUS
"FATHER OF FLIGHT."**

⋯✦⟫●⟪✦⋯

TO SOUTH AMERICA, WITH ITS ENORMOUS
distances, tremendous mountain barriers, and impene-
trable forests and jungles, the airplane came as a miracle,
bridging space and time. But South America did not
wait for men of other countries to pioneer in the air.
Brazil had its own part in giving the airplane to the
world, as travelers are reminded when, on a Pan-
American flight, they land at the fine Santos-Dumont

Airport in Rio de Janeiro. Here, on the wall of the Federal Airport building, is a huge map of Brazil, showing the many air routes which link its provinces together. All the world joined Brazil in paying honor to the pioneer airman at the time of his death in 1932, but only Brazilians went back of the famous flights in Paris at the opening of the century to the beginning of the story, to a Midwinter Day in the 1880s and a small boy at play.

On his father's coffee plantation in São Paulo a large-eyed, serious little fellow was making ready to celebrate that holiday, which we should have called Midsummer Day, for the date was June twenty-fourth. Our seasons are turned around in Brazil, and the middle of June was the coldest time of the year, so cool that in this particular year there had been frost for several nights, and great bonfires had been lighted on the edge of the coffee fields to protect the crops.

Alberto's next older brothers had gone into town to buy fireworks for this holiday, which was like our Fourth of July and also our Christmas in the manner of its celebration. Each house had in front of it a small flag with a picture of St. John, whose church festival day it was, and the street peddlers would be selling fireworks and sweet potatoes, sugar cane, and green corn to be roasted in the bonfires. For here, as on Midsum-

mer's Day in Old England, there must be fires lighted
in honor of St. John. At this turn of the year, when the
seasons changed according to the movement of the sun,
spirits were said to walk abroad, bringing good luck or
ill fortune. But the Brazilian tradition was like the English one, that if these sacred fires were lighted, they
would drive away any unwelcome spirits and so protect
the households for the coming year. Coals from the fires
would be sent to neighbors as a sign of friendliness and
good wishes.

From the table at which he sat Alberto could see the
slaves bringing wood and dry garden stuff and piling
them for the huge bonfires of Midwinter Eve. They did
it gladly, for this was the day of the year when, along
with the feasting and merrymaking, the master and mis-
tress gave new clothes to all the slaves. It was those
bonfires which Alberto had in mind. He was making
not the usual fireworks but his own playthings with
which to celebrate. For days he had been making small
silk-paper balloons and putting together little airplanes,
built of pieces of straw, with springs of twisted rubber
wound about their tails so that he could release them
and shoot them up into the air. Great currents of air
would stream up from those bonfires, and Alberto could
set off his fleets of airships in them.

Flying and engines were the two things about which

he cared. When his father and older brothers went off
on horseback to inspect distant coffee trees, he used to
go out in the fields and climb up on the seat of the
newfangled steam traction engines, with their great,
broad wheels, which his father had recently bought.
Already he was allowed to take the wheel and drive
this machine up and down the field himself. But what
he wanted to do was to drive the big Baldwin locomotive engines which brought in long trains, loaded with
green coffee berries, over the sixty-mile plantation railroad. He often rode in the cab with the engineer, and
the man had promised that when he was twelve he could
run the engine himself. Privately Alberto thought that
he could have done it now, without waiting so long.

But more even than for engines Alberto cared about
flying. The boys had been teasing him that very morning about his crazy ideas. They had been playing, as
they often did, a game which they called "Pigeon flies!"
They sat in a circle, and the leader called out rapidly
two-word sentences, such as "Pigeon flies! Hen flies!
Crow flies! Bee flies!" At each call the players raised
their fingers. The trick of the game came when, all at
once, he would call out an impossible statement, such
as "Dog flies!" or "Fox flies!" Anyone who raised a
finger then would have to pay a forfeit.

Sometimes the leader would call "Man flies!" All the others would keep their fingers down, but Alberto would always raise his hand very high and refuse to pay the forfeit. "Man does fly," he would insist, and they could not laugh him out of it.

He was thinking of this game now, as he fashioned his airplanes, trying a new shape of wing to see if he could make them carry a heavier load. He had seen pictures of a balloon with a man in its swinging car, and he had read stories of the Montgolfier brothers and some of the other early balloonists. Someday he was going up in a balloon, and someday he intended to make real airships, not play ones.

That Midwinter holiday was recalled to Alberto Santos-Dumont twenty years later. On October 19, 1901, he had made a flight which was to be famous in the history of aviation. He had flown around the Eiffel Tower during a seven-mile trip in a lighter-than-air craft of his own invention and won a prize of 100,000 francs that had been offered for such an achievement. All Paris had gone wild over the young Brazilian aviator. Thousands of letters came to him with congratulations on his success, but the one which pleased him most was from an old playmate in São Paulo. This was the way it read:

Do you remember the time, my dear Alberto, when we played together "Pigeon flies!"? It came back to me suddenly the day when the news of your success reached Rio.

"Man flies!" Old fellow, you were right to raise your finger, and you have just proved it by flying around the Eiffel Tower.

You were right not to pay the forfeit; it is M. Deutsche who has paid it in your stead. Bravo! You well deserve the 100,000-franc prize.

They play the old game more than ever at home; but the name has been changed and the rules modified since October 19, 1901. They call it now, "Man flies!", and he who does not raise his finger at the word pays his forfeit.

Your friend,
PEDRO

There was a story of long effort back of that flight, as there is behind most of the great days in men's lives. Alberto Santos-Dumont was twenty-eight years old when he made it. He was born in 1873, two years after the birth of Orville Wright. His first sight of a balloon was when he was fifteen years old, at a fair in a neighboring town where a professional balloonist was making short flights. The balloons in use for such exhibitions were spherical ones, with the gas bag shaped like a ball, and there was no attempt at steering them. The wind took them, and the only control the balloonist had was by throwing out ballast to lighten the load.

In 1891 the family made a trip to France. Senhor Henrique Santos-Dumont, Alberto's father, was a wealthy man, and it was his custom to return often to the home of his ancestors, where he in his youth had received his education as an engineer. Alberto went on that journey with two purposes. "I am going to Paris," he said to himself, "to see steerable balloons and automobiles." He had read of experiments of two inventors with balloons which they attempted to steer by means of rudders and propellers controlled by an engine, and he was eager to see the new "horseless carriages" of which people were talking.

To his surprise Alberto found that it was not much easier to get up into the air in the French capital than it had been at home. The professional balloonists to whom he went shook their heads and said that he was too young. He was only eighteen years old and looked younger than he was, for at no time in his life did he weigh more than one hundred and ten pounds, and he was slight as well as small of frame. But the costs were what made it practically impossible for anyone to get a ride.

One man finally said that he would consider taking him up, but even for an afternoon the charge would be two hundred and forty dollars, and he must sign a contract making himself responsible for a whole series of happenings. He must agree to pay for any injuries which might befall either himself or the balloonist and for any damage which might be done to either the balloon or the property of other people in case of a bad landing. He must also be responsible for the cost of transporting both the machine and its occupants back to Paris from any point in France where the wind might take them. And all this was for only a probable two or three hours in the air!

Young Santos-Dumont decided that ballooning was not to be for him at this time and devoted himself to the almost equally exciting adventure of automobiling. At the end of his stay he took home to São Paulo a car which was the wonder of the natives. Meanwhile he had learned all he could about automobile engines, gaining experience which was to serve him well when he came to build his own airships.

There were many failures before the famous October nineteenth flight. These were the years before the invention of the airplane, when most people thought flying as crazy an idea as had Alberto's childhood playmates on the São Paulo plantation. Back in Paris the young man had a little balloon of his own, the Brazil, in which he made daring and dangerous flights. Then he

began to build a new type of balloon, not round but
lengthened out to a cigar shape, with a small motor such
as those used in automobiles. These airships, which were
the forerunner of our modern airships, bore his name.
There was the Santos-Dumont No. 1, and No. 2, and so
on to the No. 6, which won the prize. He was a dare-
devil flyer, taking terrific risks, but he claimed that this
was the only way to learn. After each smash-up of his
plane he would start repairing the machine or building
a new one, either at once or as soon as he got out of
the hospital after recovering from his injuries.

Then a wealthy oil man, M. Henri Deutsche, offered
a prize of 100,000 francs to the operator of any lighter-
than-air craft who would make a flight over a seven-
mile course, encircling the Eiffel Tower and returning
to the starting point within thirty minutes. So doubtful
was it that anyone could accomplish this feat that the
man allowed five years for the attempt. It could be made
in any one of the years 1900, 1901, 1902, 1903, or 1904.

Santos-Dumont began trying for it in July of 1901,
rounding the Tower successfully on his first trip but
being delayed by a head wind and coming down in the
branches of a horse-chestnut tree on an estate near Paris.
There a curious thing happened. He must have felt himself very far from his Brazilian home, but while he
worked on his machine, up there in the tree, there came

a servant with a luncheon sent by Comtesse d'Eu, the former Princess Isabel, who was daughter of Don Pedro II, Brazil's emperor for more than half a century. She invited him to come and tell her the story of the flight. Santos-Dumont told later how she said to him:

"Your evolutions in the air make me think of the flight of our great birds of Brazil. I hope that you will do as well with your propeller as they do with their wings, and that you will succeed for the glory of our common country!"

It was good for the young Brazilian to have this word of encouragement, for he had another failure ahead of him. In August he made an attempt, but his balloon developed a leak and he was forced down over a hotel in Paris. There is a curious old photograph of him clinging to the window sill of the courtyard wall, several stories above the ground, with the balloon of the airship in tatters below him while he waited for firemen to rescue him. But he went at once about building another airship, and in this Santos-Dumont No. 6 he made the successful flight on October 19, 1901, covering the appointed distance and returning to the starting point in 29 minutes and 31 seconds, thus having only 29 seconds to spare in the required half-hour.

That was the flight which caused celebrations and rejoicings in Brazil. The government voted him a prize of one hundred *contos* (125,000 francs), which was sent to him with a beautiful gold medal, designed and cast by native artists. On its face was the figure of the airman, standing with the Eiffel Tower at his left and the rising sun at his right. He is led by a symbolic figure of Victory and is being crowned by a flying Renown who trumpets the news to the world. On the outer circle of the medal are the words which were inscribed on the long streamer floating from his airship when he made the flight, a line adapted from a Portuguese poem and meaning, "Through heavens heretofore unsailed." On the back of the gold plaque was the design of the airship, with an inscription stating that the President of the Republic of the United States of Brazil had given the order to have it made "in homage to Alberto Santos-Dumont, 19 October, 1901." The design of the ship interests us, a cigar-shaped balloon, suggesting somewhat our dirigibles, with a curious openwork basket or cradle below in which was the little motor. The story of the flight is interesting as showing one more contribution which the Americas made in the progress toward successful aviation.

Another contribution which Santos-Dumont made was the giving of publicity to the new art, or sport, as it was considered then. He was the first man to fly in Europe in public. "His airships," says an editorial in the

New York *Times* of the day of his death, July 26, 1932, "were familiar sights in France at the beginning of the century. . . . While the Wrights were still experimenting in secret, he ordered a motor-driven box kite on wheels, which was to fly tail-first. It flew, or rather hopped, and won fame, honors, prizes."

In these little monoplanes he flew often over Paris, while the people on the boulevards stood craning their necks in astonishment and admiration. More than any other flier, the dapper little South American convinced them that the airship's day had arrived. He was generous with his rides, too, remembering, doubtless, his early disappointments at being refused passage in balloons. He took boys up with him, and even young ladies, whom he allowed to manage the controls of the little gasoline engines. In these little machines he did actually make the first flights in Europe with heavier-than-air machines, the Bird of Prey, the famous Demoiselle, and the Dragon-Fly; but they were only the shortest of flights, for he had not the secrets of balancing and control which the Wrights were building into their airplanes in those same years from 1903 to 1908, the date when Wilbur Wright brought their invention to France.

Santos-Dumont's health failed in his later years, and he lived quietly much of the time in Paris, though returning to his own country from time to time. The Brazilians gave him great welcomes when he came, and at the time of his death there in 1932 a war was stopped for two days in his honor. In his native state of São Paulo there was at that time a civil war going on, but General Goes Monteiro, chief of the Federal forces, ordered his planes to cease their bombing activities and drop proclamations in São Paulo hailing the Brazilian air pioneer. When peace was restored, a few months later, the Brazilian government planned a state funeral, similar to those for presidents of the Republic, in which representatives of all nations and many flying societies joined. On that occasion a carpet of laurel leaves was spread on the Avenida Rio Branco for two hundred and seventy meters, the distance of Santos-Dumont's first flight. While airplanes saluted above, the casket was borne along this route from the Candalara Cathedral to the cemetery through crowds of reverent Brazilians, who showered the procession with white rose petals. But the honor to Santos-Dumont did not end on that day. He is remembered as his name is spoken a hundred times a day, while planes come and go at the Santos-Dumont Airport of Rio de Janeiro.

Over the Uspallata Pass

FROM FOOTPATH TO TUNNEL TO AIRWAY

AT NO SINGLE SPOT ON THE SOUTH
American continent can the steps of man's conquest of
the Andes be seen more clearly than at the famous
Uspallata Pass between Chile and Argentina.

Indians of the days before the coming of the white
men climbed along a narrow path, perhaps with llamas
with them, carrying their loads. These "little camels" of
the Andes were the only burden bearers the Incas had

233

in the four hundred years when they were extending their empire from Peru to Chile and northward to Quito. These animals could live at altitudes of over two and a half miles above sea level, where in later days the horses and mules, brought by the conquerors, would die of mountain sickness.

Over their roads, if a "llama path" or a mule path can be called a road, a single explorer or two or three traders went now and again in the days of the conquistadors. But the traveled route across the continent was farther north, across from Peru to Upper Peru (now Bolivia) and then down to Buenos Aires. The southern Andes practically shut the door between Chile and Argentina.

Then came the days of independence. San Martín and his army had followed Chilean muleteers and miners in making the journey. Charles Darwin could go across with a guide. There were the little stone huts at intervals along the mountain ways which Don Ambrosio O'Higgins had built, where travelers could stop when caught by darkness or a storm. Then there were the mailmen of the later years of the nineteenth century, "Postmen of the Snows." By this time there was a stage, or diligence, during the summer months when the pass was open. Travelers tell of this Andean, or Andine, stage, which held four passengers comfortably, six if they were packed close. The road had been widened so that four horses could go along abreast, and the driver swung them around the zigzag turns. The stage stopped running in the middle of May, the beginning of the southern winter. But the "Postmen of the Snows" kept on, riding their mules or horses along the stage route. They carried their mail in leather bags, strapped to their backs. Their feet were covered with sheepskin footgear, with fur next to the skin, the upper parts fastened to a very thick leather sole, and the whole bound to the leg by thongs of leather. Woolen trousers, a poncho, a stick with a steel point, and a small bag with rations of dried meat, biscuit, and onions completed the outfit of these men who braved cold and storms to carry the mail across the Andes. The skin on their faces was toughened till it was almost like leather, but their eyes were bright and their chins strong. They were men to marvel at, as they went with no talk or question about their government task.

Then spring would come, and a thousand cattle would be sent across to break the trail. Many of them would die in the high altitudes, but enough would get across to leave a wide, hard road. Once more the stages could get through with their passengers.

Next, railroads began to climb up the lower slopes. The mountain resisted them, as it does to this day.

(Snowslides and avalanches wiped out, in 1934, part of the track.) But again men would not be halted. A tunnel through the mountain, below the Uspallata Pass, was begun. Wheelwright had dreamed of a Trans-andine Railway and taken the first steps toward its building on the Chilean side. Two Chilean brothers, Juan and Mateo Clark, had built in the 1880s from the Argentine side. The tunnel was to be 2500 feet below the Cumbre Pass, as the Simplon Tunnel had been cut through the Swiss mountains.

In 1909 the work was completed. Coming from Caracole on the Chilean side and Las Cuevas on the Argentine, the workmen had met in the middle, far below the mountain pass. The cut was only ninety yards short of two miles. An Italian workman, a man who had worked on Alpine tunnels, had the honor of breaking out the last thin wall of rock that separated the two cuts. The first man to go through from east to west was the chief of the Argentinean workmen, and ninety of his men went with him. Many of them were Chileans who were returning to their native soil by this new underground route which they had helped to build. This was on November 27, 1909. In May of 1910, when Argentina was celebrating the hundredth anniversary of its Declaration of Independence, there came the official opening, with ceremonies of rejoicing as officials of Argentina and Chile made the journey back and forth and saw their two countries more closely united.

But the closest union was still to come, the crossing of the Andes at this point by airplane. Jorge Chávez, a Peruvian, had planned it, but he crashed to his death in Italy after making the first successful airplane flight over the Alps. A faulty landing smashed his plane, the parts of which are still on exhibition in a public building in Lima. That was in 1908. By 1912 other airmen were practicing to make the flight at that terrific height.

Jorge Newbury, an Argentinean, who held in 1913 the altitude record for South America, made careful studies, covering a period of many months, of the atmospheric conditions over the mountains and the best routes. He started from Mendoza on the first day of March in 1914, but an accident to his plane, shortly afterward, brought it to earth and him to his death.

A Chilean who had won many South American records for distance and speed made three attempts to cross by the Uspallata Pass, but his engine was not equal to lifting him to the required height.

Then, in 1916, two Argentineans, Captain Zuloaga, of the national army, and his engineer by the name of Bradley, won their victory over the mountains in a balloon, taking off on the Chilean side and landing near

Mendoza less than four hours later. It was a magnificent achievement for those times, a victory commemorated by a tablet erected in the mountain pass over which they flew.

Airplane motors were improved, so that they could carry heavier loads to great heights, and crossings were made from east to west and west to east during the year 1918. But the marvel of that Transandine flight does not grow less as the years go by. To every traveler who journeys above the peaks in one of the modern planes the wonder is renewed. Still the mountains are approached with caution. A radio station in the Uspallata Pass gives weather reports before the planes are allowed to start. But when they do go, the crossing is made in a little over an hour. The planes from the Chilean side, starting at Santiago, come down in Mendoza, where the great monument to San Martín stands, with the southern Liberator standing with eyes uplifted to the mountains over which he laboriously took his victorious army.

With Pen and Sword —Sarmiento

THE STORY OF THE "SCHOOLMASTER
PRESIDENT" OF ARGENTINA

THERE COMES A TIME IN THE HISTORY OF
a country when the kind of pioneering which is needed
changes. Mountains and rivers and deserts are not the
only obstacles, nor kings and viceroys sent from overseas, the only dangers to freedom. The man who was
to be called the "schoolmaster president" was born in
1811 and lived until 1888. Those seventy-seven years
covered the change in Argentina from a colony of the

Spanish empire to a full-grown nation, and Domingo Faustino Sarmiento was active at every stage of that transformation.

He was born six years before General San Martín took his army over the Andes, spending his early years in a humble farming home near San Juan on one of the slopes of the mountains not very far distant from the passes that led over into Chile. His father was one of San Martín's soldiers, and his mother was a strong, beautiful, patriotic woman. The patriots believed in the education of children as the only way to democracy and freedom. Before they fought, in the midst of their campaigns, and after their victories it was their first concern to set up schools and start libraries. In the year when little Domingo was five such a school was started in the town near which the Sarmiento family lived, and the ambitious father and mother sent their boys to it.

Nine years of schooling under an able patriot master gave Domingo his start. Yet he seems not to have liked school very well, except for that proud moment when, by a democratic choice, he was made "First Citizen" and allowed to sit on a platform above his fellow pupils and carry on the school government for the time. When he became "First Citizen" of the republic of Argentina, that picture of the little boy mounted on his high chair was remembered.

Sarmiento's real education he won for himself, and one of our own American heroes started him on the way to it. Indeed, this Argentinean seems like one of our famous men, with his struggle for education and his rise to high office. It was when he was fourteen or fifteen years old, earning his own living in a country store, that he found this hero of ours. School was behind him, and he felt utterly alone in a world where he must spend his time selling groceries and measuring yards of cloth. But he knew there was a world of books, and he rushed out to find something to read. He came upon the *Life of Benjamin Franklin* and was comforted and started on his path.

"No book," he wrote later, "has ever done me more good. . . . I felt myself to be like Franklin—and why not? I was very poor like him, I studied like him, and, following in his footsteps, I might one day come, like him, to be a *doctor ad honorem,* and to make myself a place in letters and American politics."

It is a thoroughly American picture that we have of this boy, reading every book he could get hold of, reading after he had swept out the store, reading while he sold herbs and sugar, and wishing that customers would not come in to call him away from an exciting chapter in a book. He read Greek and Roman history and Cicero, and began to think about freedom and government.

That interest meant disaster to anyone who did not accept the rule of the government. This was the period of *caudillos* in South America, "strong men" who took control of provinces or republics in the unsettled times following the winning of independence and ruled well or ill according to their ideas and tempers. Quiroga, who was in authority in this region at the time, was a tyrant, brutal and unreasonable in his rule. When a revolution was started against him, young Sarmiento took an active part. Many of his intimate boyhood friends were caught and executed when the rising was put down, but young Sarmiento suffered only imprisonment. Even that period was not too unhappy, for he was kept in a private house where there was a library of French books, and a good-natured French soldier taught him the language. This was the first of the languages which he mastered in amazingly short periods during these early years.

Neither he nor his family could safely remain in the province of San Juan. They escaped with many other patriots to Chile, and there he tried his hand at school-teaching, running an eating house, and working in a store, to earn his living. It was while he was working in Valparaiso that he found an Englishman who would teach him English. Sarmiento's pay for a month was an ounce of silver. He divided this in two and paid half to the English professor for his lessons, giving, also, two small coins of what remained to a night watchman who waked him every week night at two o'clock in the morning for his studies. In six weeks, with constant study on Saturdays and Sundays added, he had mastered English so that he could read it easily, though he still could not pronounce.

Fortune favored him, and he got a job as foreman in one of the silver mines. There he found other young men who were in exile like himself. They used to get together nightly in a kitchen of one of their number and talk politics and discuss the future of their country. One would have liked to see the future president of Argentina dressed in the costume of a Chilean miner, with doublet, hose, striped trousers, red cap, and broad sash. The evenings were not all serious. His friends found that Sarmiento could draw and made him entertain them by drawing pictures of birds and animals. He also discovered a set of the works of Sir Walter Scott and turned his newly acquired knowledge of English to use by reading a book a day until he was through, reveling in the first romantic stories he had ever met.

The tyrant Quiroga was assassinated in 1835, and Sarmiento went back to his home town. The next glimpse of him is in a government position, making his first public address. He had helped to start a school for girls, a most progressive venture in that country where girls had been kept strictly in their homes. Now he opened the school with an encouraging address, telling of the blessings of education, even though the beginnings were always "disagreeable and troublesome." Here he became for the first time a newspaper editor, beginning a work which he was to continue with one paper after another for much of the rest of his life. Of course, being the kind of young man he was, he attacked the evils of the government and got himself into trouble by expressing radical views. But one wonders whether anyone of even moderately advanced views could have been safe long in Argentina at that time. At any rate, young Sarmiento was soon going over the Andes again into Chile, where there was, fortunately, a liberal government in power.

He had been imprisoned, beaten, and ordered out of his town, but before he left he gave himself the satisfaction of writing in charcoal on a prominent wall of a building words from a French philosopher, "Ideas cannot have their throats cut." In Chile, Manuel Montt, then Minister of Education, who was to be his fast friend and supporter, met him with the saying, "Ideas, sir, have no country."

Chile gave him his chance, and Sarmiento responded with his best gifts of service. He founded a Normal School, said to be the first one established on American soil, edited liberal papers, and was appointed to the chair of Philosophy and Letters when the University of Chile was established. But while he accepted college honors, his interest was in children. He wrote primary-school textbooks, which were sadly needed, and started new programs for secondary schools.

He went to Europe to study educational methods and spent years going from place to place, meeting the leading writers and thinkers in France, Spain, and Italy, and going over to England, where he heard about the educational work which was being done in the United States by Horace Mann. Nothing would do but he must see this other American and find out what he was doing. He crossed the ocean, visited Mr. Mann, and became his fast friend. When he went back to South America he was convinced that education was the only road to good government in the troubled republics.

"Give me the department of schools," he said; "this is the future of the republics."

By this time he was an author as well as an editor, having written his famous book *Facundo*, which pictures Argentine life on the pampas in that period and sketches the life of a *caudillo* ruler. Sarmiento put his educational ideas into practice in Chile and then was able to go back to Argentina, to his own town from which he had been three times banished. Now he had a chance to fight with both pen and sword, for an army was raised to fight the dictator Rosas, against whom he had been working for the years of his exile. He proved himself an able fighter, rising to the rank of colonel in the army. But his service from now on was to be of another sort. He was chosen for offices in Buenos Aires where he could work for his beloved school system.

During these years and in the period of his presidency he exerted his powerful influence for public schools. The list of his public offices is long. He came here to the United States as Minister from Argentina and was only recalled from Washington by his election, during his absence, to the presidency. It was during his stay in this country that he made an interesting address before the Rhode Island Historical Society, in which he told of having visited his friend William Wheelwright in the tent where, with map and compass, he was tracing out railroads to reach other hundreds of miles across the country.

With a characteristic touch of wit, he mentions the Newburyport gentleman as the "contractor of railways

which are carrying to the pampas the civilizing snort
of the locomotive, where formerly the neighing of
horses alone was heard." With pardonable pride he
tells of the changes that would be noted by those who
had visited the country only ten or twenty years earlier.
Cities were becoming beautiful; roads were connecting
the separated regions; and, first, last, and always, schools
were being built and free libraries established. As
President, he had money from the sale of public lands
turned to the building and equipping of schoolhouses
all over the country. He brought a group of trained
teachers from the United States to start the new system.
Nor did he neglect the education of the older groups
because of his enthusiasm for children. The Military
Academy and Naval School was created at Cordoba,
and the world-famous Observatory founded, to which
scholars from the United States and elsewhere came.

In his crusading for his causes he has been compared
with our own Theodore Roosevelt. The two men did
have much in common. Sarmiento was a writer from
whose pen came one book after another, even during
his busiest years. In Washington he took great pleasure
in writing a life of Lincoln for his people. In all, there
were fifty-three volumes to his credit at the time of his
death. Like Theodore Roosevelt, he had a tremendous
interest in all sorts of things. At the time when he

seemed entirely absorbed in railways and schools and
libraries he was sending a courier to Chile for willow
trees to be planted on an island in the Parana River
to which he often journeyed. Every planter was presented with a twig from these trees, as an encouragement to making the island more beautiful.

Most of all, he pioneered in ideas. The age of the
Gaucho was passing. The half-civilized, picturesque
Spanish-Indians, who roamed the pampas on their
horses, herding their cattle, must become settled citizens.
The "Sovereign People" must rule. That was his creed.
But if they were to rule, the "Sovereign People must be
educated." Among many strong and able leaders who
made Argentina a modern nation, the "Schoolmaster
President" is honored today for his tremendous devo-
tion to that creed.

Pioneering
on Other Fronts

WITH A LOOK AHEAD

PIONEERING CHANGES, BUT IT NEVER
ends. There are always new frontiers. Those of the
twentieth century are different from those of earlier
days, but there is still the challenge to men of faith and
courage.

In 1902 there came to Paris, to the famous Pasteur
Institute, a committee of Brazilian officials seeking advice and help. In Havana, Cuba, following the Amer-

ican occupation of the island, yellow fever was being wiped out. That was headline news in the tropics, where the dread disease took a terrible toll every year. These men were from Rio de Janeiro, the capital of Brazil, a city with one of the finest harbors in the world, where ships should be coming and going constantly. But during its frequent epidemics of yellow fever it was shunned by all shipping. Every known measure of preventing the disease had been tried without success. The people lived in constant fear of new outbreaks of the trouble. At that very moment there was a serious epidemic under way.

A new President, Rodrigues Alves, had been elected in Brazil. He had sent these men to the Parisian center of medical learning to find a French scientist to lead in a crusade for health. What was being done in Havana should be attempted in Rio.

"But you need not call in a foreigner," the director of the Pasteur Institute told these gentlemen. "Your own fellow countryman, Dr. Oswaldo Cruz, who has been with us for years, has been experimenting along these very lines. You could find no one better than this young man from your own capital to go back with you."

So Oswaldo Cruz, then thirty years old, returned to his native land after nearly ten years of study and research in Paris. No one knew better than he the horror of this disease. His father, a distinguished physician of Rio, had served during the last years of his life as director-general of hygiene for the entire region. He had told the boy of the first great epidemic in 1849, when more than four thousand people died. Since then no year had been free of the disease, and in some years there had been many hundreds of deaths. Young Cruz had heard abroad the saying in shipping circles, "to go to Rio is to commit suicide." It was because of this knowledge that he had followed with interest and excitement the news from Cuba and had worked out experiments along these lines in his Parisian laboratory.

Returning, the young doctor found in President Alves a chief with whom he could work; and the President found, to his comfort, a man who spoke with confidence.

"Give me the proper backing, a sufficient force of men, and the needed money, and I will rid Rio of yellow fever in three years," the young doctor said, and President Alves listened and took courage.

Dr. Cruz organized a brigade of seventy-five physicians, who would work with him. Then he went to the colleges and told the students his plans, and large numbers of them enlisted with enthusiasm for the service. A big company of laborers was hired to work under their direction. This army of crusaders then spread itself out over the big city in the manner of a modern money-raising campaign, but theirs was more than a task of ringing doorbells and making requests. They must do the work which had to be done.

Rio was a city of nearly 700,000 people, an old city with many narrow streets and alleys next door to the beautiful wide avenues which were being constructed in its central parts. Following the method used by the United States pioneers, Dr. Cruz had set as goal that there should not be left a single open tank, gutter, fish-pond, or other spot with standing water in which the disease-bearing mosquitos might breed. In one year nearly 1,500,000 reservoirs and tanks were cleaned, and they were kept clean. The vigilant army of watchers saw to that. Hundreds upon hundreds of houses must be disinfected. Cruz's young men went out with huge sail-cloths with which they covered the roofs and blocked the chimneys, while sulphur vapor was doing its work in the sealed rooms below.

People protested, but the Congress passed laws giving the workers the needed authority. The press ridiculed these violent measures, but the doctor and his army of followers went calmly on. It was unpleasant work, and it seemed never-ending. Day after day, week after week, the gutters on the roofs of hundreds of buildings were cleaned out. Ponds known to be breeding places for the mosquitoes were stocked with tiny fish of a kind known to hunt and devour the insects. Half measures would be of no use. That was what Dr. Cruz was constantly preaching. The work must be complete to be effective.

The people came to accept the cleaning up of the city, though they grumbled. But when the question came of treating such cases of the disease as occurred, the battle was on between the old methods of treatment, built on the old theories of the cause of the disease, and Dr. Cruz's new, simple methods. Public protests were made against the innovations by this "rash young man," and his recall from his high post was demanded. President Alves himself was disturbed by the rising tide of indignation. He called Dr. Cruz to him and asked if, in order to calm the people, it might not be well to keep on with some of the old methods of treatment, combining them with the new.

"The Government is within its rights to follow its own views and act according to the advice of political leaders," replied Dr. Cruz. "But so long as I remain Director General of Public Health, I shall not use any medical means in the treatment of disease which is not according to my best scientific convictions."

"But are you sure of the results?" asked the President.

"If at the end of three years the epidemics have not disappeared from Rio de Janeiro," declared the doctor, "I demand to be hung in the public square."

There was no more question of turning back to the old ways.

As the race with time went on, there began to be encouragement in the health bulletins as they were made public. In 1902, the year before the work began, there had been 984 deaths from the disease. At the end of 1903 the number had been cut to 584. In 1904 there were only 48 deaths. After that the numbers decreased, with only the few cases where men came into the city from ships or from infected regions. Soon there were no deaths. Dr. Cruz had made good his promise. He had accomplished the most spectacular feat in medical history for a city of that size.

The news of his achievement spread through Brazil. Other regions took up the work. He was called to repeat his project in the city of Belém, capital of the state of Pará, to the north at the mouth of the Amazon River. There his record was by months instead of years. In Rio an Institute of Tropical Diseases was set up, where serums and vaccines were prepared. That institute now bears his name. As one reads of Dr. Cruz's work, one wonders if he had an inner urge to work fast because his time was to be short. He died on February

11, 1917, at the age of forty-four. By that time he had become a world figure, honored for his public health work abroad as well as at home.

The fight against yellow fever was the sign of a new kind of pioneering, one with no national boundaries. Scientists in Cuba, the United States, and Brazil contributed to the achievement. The benefits belonged to all the Americas, with the successful building of the Panama Canal as a direct result. Other battles against disease are today being fought by the scientists of many republics, in North America and South America alike, men whose names are becoming equally well known.

No pioneering of the past has come to a complete end in South America. Exploring is not finished. Within recent years long-lost ancient cities, buried for centuries under a cover of green vegetation, have been brought to view. In the Amazon basin there are great regions which are little known. Scientists go into these places in search for herbs and plants for the healing of disease.

There is still the search for treasure, never more intense than in our own day when minerals and raw products are precious as they never were before. The tin of Bolivia and the oil deposits of Venezuela and Colombia are as much desired as were the mines of Inca gold and silver.

The great distances remain, but the airplane is accomplishing the work begun by Bolívar and San Martín of making the continent a unit. Yet the nations, large and small, are separate, as the nations of Europe have always been separate. The ambitions and problems of each nation differ from those of the neighbor country beyond the mountains or rivers or across the plains. Some republics have very large numbers of dark-skinned native peoples, who must become the citizens of the future. There must be a steady battle against ignorance and poverty and disease throughout the countries of South America as there is in all of North America. Wide-open spaces have attracted, within the past seventy-five years, large numbers of settlers from overseas. These must be brought into the life of the republics. Modern industry is bringing labor problems. Foreign markets, on which trade depends, are being lost or won according to the sweep of the tide of war beyond the oceans.

The story of the past gives abundant promise for the future. South Americans won their continent against many odds. The leaders of the present are as ready as were the men of the past to move forward and establish on firmer foundations that which has been won with such courage and vision.

Index

Index

꙳꙳꙳꙳꙳꙳꙳꙳꙳꙳꙳꙳꙳

263